A RELUCTANT CIVIL SERVANT

By

JIM O'SHEA

First Edition
Published 2011

© 2011 JIM O'SHEA

ISBN 978-1-908784-00-1

British Library Cataloguing in Publication Data

A catalogue record for this book is available from the British Library
The publishers have made every reasonable effort to contact the copyright holders of photographs and texts reproduced in this book. If any involuntary infringement of copyright has occurred, sincere apologies are offered and the owners of such copyright are requested to contact the
publishers

Cover photograph - Original Painting of Ballykeanan Lock, River Barrow
by Jim O'Shea

Published by PUBLISHME.IE

Printed and Bound by Dundalk Bookbinding

Foreword

The Border or land frontier was introduced on the 1st April 1923. Revenue officials from both jurisdictions took up duties from that date.

This came to an end on the 1st January 1993 with the introduction of the Single Market which dispensed with the need for border protection. The Customs and Excise Service seemed to be airbrushed into oblivion. Today as you drive on the M1 from Dublin to Belfast there is nothing in sight to remind you of that land frontier.

I had been retired for a number of years when I joined with Donal Cotter, a Colleague, who was researching the history of the Preventive Service in the Dundalk area. Donal had been active for a considerable time and had an amount of important material on hand. We continued this research for a number of years and were surprised to find that some official records were not available having been mislaid or destroyed. This left a big gap in our documentation.

About this time we attended computer lessons. Geoff Carolan was our tutor. We mentioned bits of our story during breaks in the class. Geoff seemed to take an interest in our venture.

The work on the story continued but in time it became haphazard and came to an end. Donal told me that I was free to use the material we had accumulated as I wished. The story got a rest.

My family suggested enlarging the story to include my life story. I agreed and emphasized that it would be just a story. They arranged for me to meet Davy Donohoe and after some time we had the foundation of a story on paper. I wish to acknowledge Davy's contribution. Again the story was given a rest.

It was resurrected some considerable time later when I had the good luck to meet Geoff. He enquired about the story's progress. Offering to help he encouraged me to make the effort and finish the job. We produced an extemporized version of the story. Finally, I wish to thank Noel Ross for his help and advice in proof reading this book.

DEDICATION

This book is dedicated to my wife Joan who died on the
19th September 1992

Table of Contents:

1 | GROWING UP IN GRAIGNAMANAGH.

B orn in 1921, I was the eldest of six, three boys and three girls. My parents were Pierce and Anastasia, or 'Pierry' and 'Stass' as they were known to their friends. Myself (Jim), Mick and Harry made up the boys. Mairead, Kitty and Carmel were the girls. Harry, the youngest, stayed at home, looking after our parents until they passed on. Since then Harry and his wife Maureen kept an open house for the family. We all enjoyed the continuing hospitality in Graig. Years later, all six of us got together frequently at the Gresham Hotel, Dublin to mark some special events. Sadly at the time of going to print, there are only three of us remaining alive. Harry, Mick and Kitty having died over the last three years. We lived in a terraced house on Abbey Street in Graignamanagh, right beside the 'Duiske' Abbey. Founded in 1204, Duiske Abbey started away back years ago as one of the biggest Cistercian monasteries in the country and there has been a continuity of worship there for the last 800 years. The word Duiske is a corruption of Dubh Uisce which means Blackwater referring to a river that flows into the river Barrow in Graignamanagh. The monks that settled there originally came from England and because of this Norman influence they were unable to pronounce Dubh Uisce and so referred to the location as Duiske. The Abbey was a special place for all the people in the town and I was an altar boy there for many years until I went to the secondary school.

All of my father's family, including my grandfather, were in the painting and decorating business. In fact one of my earliest memories is sitting on my father's knee and getting the smell of paint. I later remember him washing his hands and cleaning his nails. His strict hygiene was doubly required back then as lead was the base for most paints at that time. I remember the cooking arrangements; some of it was done on an open fire and some done in an oven which was heated by a paraffin contraption. Later the arrival of a 'Stanley' coal-fed cooker made things easier and was a very welcome addition to the kitchen. I recall my mother always insisted on a full coal shed in advance of winter.

At the age of three I was sent to a Convent of Mercy infant's school a short bit up the road from our house. A lady called Ms. Curran was the teacher there. A gentle lady, she made everybody feel at home because it was their first time going to school. I remember she had a bamboo cane with a handle, which sat on the table in front of her. This initially frightened the children but we soon learned that the only time she ever used the cane was to scratch her back! She taught at the school for forty years.

After infant's school the next move was to Graignamanagh National School which was a mixed school run by nuns. After my first communion I was transferred to the boy's school. The boy's school was very old and had just three teachers – Mr. Coonan, the principal, a very strict, unkind individual, Mr. Hogan and Mr. Grace, a local man who was poor on discipline but a very good teacher nonetheless. Mr. Grace's favourite hobby was inventing nicknames for the boys in his class and mine was 'Dauber', because my family were painters and decorators. In return we decided to create a nickname for Mr. Grace and came up with 'Wax'. He had a brother who was a shoemaker and wax was the substance used to waterproof the stitching on shoes and boots at that time. Oddly Mr. Grace never had his lunch with the other teachers. His house-keeper would come up with the basket and he would eat alone in a galvanised shed out the back. Myself and the boys often wondered about this so one day we decided to investigate. We crept up to the shed and through a small hole in the metal we peered in at Mr. Grace. There he was, with his clay pipe in hand, smoking away to his heart's content! The mystery was solved.

After school most days we would occupy ourselves by playing marbles and hoops which were made by taking the spokes and axle out of old bicycle wheels. We also played hurling of course and would hit balls up against stone walls, shed doors and up and down the street. During the winter, when hurling wasn't an option, we would make ice slides on the road.

Sometime after I arrived at the old boy's school we were relocated to a new, purpose-built school on the Wood Road. Everything was shiny and new and we were the first batch to be taught there. The only problem was that the toilet was located thirty yards outside of the school. That was Office of Public Works thinking in those days. The school was in a lovely location looking down on the River Barrow and had a wonderful view of the bridge. Interestingly, during the 1798 Rebellion, two arches of the bridge had been blown up. The bridge spanned the River Barrow from Graignamanagh all the way across to Tinnahinch, which was where my grandfather on my mother's side, Mick Maguire, lived. From this view we could see across the river to County Carlow and right below us the 'Sandys', a stretch of shallow water with a sandy bottom where we did all our swimming as children. My father always supervised me swimming but across the way on the County Carlow side, you would often see a man called Eddie Power swimming, he was a retired teacher and a bit of a poet as I recall. Eddie would act as an unofficial lifeguard of sorts during the summer months.

Granny O'Shea & Jim 1923.

Life did have its ups and downs though. The 1920's and 30's were a tough period for the country. We had to be satisfied with a life with few luxuries. T.B. was rampant and entire families had been wiped out. Graignamanagh was also subject to outbreaks of diphtheria causing loss of life. We were friendly with the Doyle family and my brother Mick had visited Mark Doyle every day when he became ill. Liam and Carmel Doyle also caught the infection. I remember my father asking Dr O'

Brien to go back and re-examine Mick's throat as he said he saw something unusual. Lucky for Mick he was transferred to the fever hospital in Kilkenny just in time. I had shared a bed with Mick but luckily escaped the illness. We had to vacate our house and have it fumigated. I went to stay with my grandmother O'Shea where I was very well treated or spoiled to be more accurate. Mick recovered and had no ill effects for the rest of his life. Liam Doyle got the diphtheria but also survived to live a normal life and joined the defence forces with me in 1940. A modern sewerage system was subsequently introduced which helped eliminate the diphtheria problem.

Mr. Coonan, the principal, was a very good teacher but, in contrast to Mr. Grace, he was a real disciplinarian. He would use the cane a lot, belting the hell out of most of us for the least little thing. For the most part I managed to avoid being hit however there was one poor lad in particular who would get hammered everyday over homework. The lad's mother had passed away sometime earlier and we decided this wasn't right so we began wondering how we would get back at Coonan. One day after a few of us had been hit we devised a plan. Every year an external diocesan examiner, a priest, would arrive to examine the school students in religious doctrine and hymn singing. We also knew that Mr. Coonan was very conscious of getting a good mark from him. The day before the examiner was due to arrive Mr. Coonan was preparing us at hymn rehearsal. We had decided not to co-operate and so when asked to sing we simply spoke the lines instead. Knowing something was up, Mr. Coonan instructed us to sing the 'solfège' (musical scale) 'Do Re Mi,' again we defiantly spoke the notes instead. Mr. Coonan was furious, but he knew that if we repeated our protest in front of the examining priest it would reflect badly on his school. The next day, to Mr. Coonan's relief, when the examiner arrived we sang at our best and delivered the hymns perfectly. Our protest had been successful, Mr. Coonan's use of the cane eased off considerably after that.

There was a lot of pressure in Mr. Coonan's class which affected me at times. I remember getting headaches and at lunchtime, instead of going into the kitchen to eat, I'd go straight up to bed. My mother would draw the curtains for me and leave me alone. Apparently I was suffering from migraine attacks but luckily I grew out of these by the time I moved on to Thomastown. In later life these attacks revisited me for a period and were still unpleasant.

Principal Coonan sent me down to the Convent school with a message for one of the nuns and with explicit instructions to deliver the message in Irish. So I went down, knocked at the door, but handed her the message instead and returned to my class. Sometime afterwards Mr. Coonan obviously got talking to the nun and found out that no Irish was spoken because I was sent back the following day and again told to speak in Irish to her. I went to the Convent again, this time to the senior class in which I had an older cousin, and I was brought up to the front of the class to carry on a conversation 'as Gaeilge' with the nun. This ended up being more than a 'cúpla focal' and went on for some time. My cousin told my aunt Mollie, who was a school teacher, about my 'fluent' display of Irish. This pleased her immensely as she was very fond of the language, so much so that each summer she would travel down to a Gaeltacht, Ring College in Waterford, to brush up. She even told me that her father, my grandfather, tried to teach himself Irish at one time. I'm almost certain that this was instrumental in my aunt taking an interest in my further education.

During the summertime we would entertain ourselves by boating, fishing and swimming on the River Barrow. If you could swim across the river from the Kilkenny side to the Carlow side, you were recognised as a swimmer which I did for the first time when I was nine. After that, my father allowed me to swim in the deeper spots which are still marked today by a well-known rock, the 'Devils Eyebrow', just north of Graignamanagh.

Mick, Harry and Jim.

Jim, Liam Doyle and Willy Doran.

11

I remember one particular summer day, Hazel Doyle, a friend of the family, took a few of us on a boat trip up the river through the lock gates to a place called Clashganny. Hazel's father had married twice and she was of the first. The whole afternoon was spent picnicking on what we called the 'Island', a piece of land between the canal and the river. We set up the grub there, went fishing and even caught a couple of nice brown trout. I always remember that trip to this day and look back on it with fond memories. Years afterwards myself and Hazel's brother, Liam Doyle, who was a friend of mine throughout my childhood, would join the army together.

Graignamanagh itself was a boating place, in that, there was no railway or fleet of lorries to transport goods from one place to another in the early 1930s so, the Grand Canal, which ran through Graignamanagh, was in full use at that time. My mother's people were into the boats which would ply between Graignamanagh, New Ross and Waterford. Every weekday, barges would come through loaded with coal, beer, grain, flour and sugar beet. Odlums had a flour mill in St Mullins and would use the barges to bring in grain and transport their flour to various destinations around the country.

The River Barrow, which ran as far as St Mullins, was tidal. Boats would wait at St Mullins for the tide to turn, and when it did it would take them all the way to Waterford. As the saying goes, 'time and tide waits for no man'. There was one privately owned boat operating on the Barrow while I was growing up called the 'Coolawn'. It was part of the social life of the town as apart from conveying selective cargo it was the centre piece of the annual regatta being used for both the diving and greasy pole events. The local brass band would also be on board providing the music. The 'Pattern' in St Mullins was celebrated every summer and was attended by people from Carlow, Kilkenny and Wexford. The Graignamanagh contingent would travel on board the Coolawn accompanied by the brass band and all would gather to celebrate the hero's of '98.

My grandfather had a boat on the river prior to the arrival of the Grand Canal Company, who eventually took over the running of the canals from the Barrow Navigation Company. One of my grandfather's boats was actually the last boat to be built in 'The Docks', a boat-building yard based in Graignamanagh. I often look back with regret that no part of that boat was kept for posterity.

At the time there was some type of a deal done when the Grand Canal Company took over from the Barrow Navigation Company. I know that on my grandmother's side they got a lock house and grazing rights. Soon after, my grandfather, in conjunction with his brother-in-law Jim Kinsella, became involved in manning the lock in Ballykeenan, just north of Graignamanagh.

This lock my grandfather operated was a two-chamber lock, the only two-chamber lock on the Grand Canal. Because of the steepness of the river, north of Graignamanagh, a two-chamber lock was needed with three gates. Many a time I went up to work the locks, even filling in for my Uncle John on one occasion when he was sick. Because I was big enough at the time and it was during the holiday period I was able to take over the opening of the gates and supervise the canal boats going through. A beautiful location I would paint the scene many years later on canvas.

The lock-keeper's house, Graignamanagh.

Each Sunday, through my uncle's lock, a precious cargo of Guinness would pass on its way from Dublin to Waterford. It was said at the time that the Guinness travelled better on the water rather than being shunted around on a train when being transported. Well by the time the boat had passed through the two chambers the boat-men were able to bore a hole in the side of the timber barrels and draw out a couple of buckets for local consumption. The occasional bucket of Guinness that wouldn't be missed was another perk for the lock-keeper, and one that made the Guinness a very welcome, and a much anticipated cargo in Graignamanagh.

Digressing, my uncle John was about the best read man around the place, he read everything. My aunt Mollie also possessed a wealth of knowledge of the local history. I've lamented every day I didn't get her on tape. In later years I tried to get her to record some of the stories, however each time I asked her she'd reply with the same excuse, 'my old rusty voice' so I didn't push her. It was an education to listen to herself and John as we drove around this historic region. She would be able to tell me the history of a place, but my uncle would always be at hand to correct her as he was a slightly better authority on such matters.

My grandfather, Mick Maguire who died in 1925, had two grown-up sons. One of them Jimmy, continued working with the boats while the other, John, who also continued to help manage the lock, set up the town's first hackney service with one of the earliest cars in Graignamanagh. I often got a spin in the car to Tramore beach, which would, years later, retire to rest on stilts in the garage.

The 1932 Elections

The thirties were a turbulent time being so soon after the Civil War. We were approaching the famous 1932/33 elections. My father, an old I.R.A. man who was not involved in the Civil War had recently joined Fianna Fail. He had me out early putting up posters for the Fianna Fail candidates, Tom Derricg, Sean Gibbons and Dr. Humphries. I remember that Desmond Fitzgerald and Dinny Gorey, who was a local farmer, were the two candidates for Fine Gael or Cumann Na gael as they were known back then, and that Pattison was the Labour man that year.

14

All the political meetings were held in a big open space quite close to where I lived, down at the junction of Main St. and Abbey St. In those days the candidates and their entourage would mount a platform or flat bottomed lorry and address an assembled crowd. One evening there was a meeting, and the gathered crowd, mainly women in shawls, started heckling the Cumann Na gael candidate. Cumann Na gael were extremely unpopular at the time as they had taken a shilling off the old-age pensioners and the crowd were not going to let them forget it. Dinny Gorey, the Cumann Na gael candidate, stood up to speak. He used to keep greyhounds and so each time he tried to address the crowd the women would begin barking like greyhounds, in an effort to interrupt him and get under his skin. After a few minutes and failing to deliver his speech, he departed the stage irritably shouting, 'will ye shut up the lot'a ya, you're like a lot of bullin heifers!' The parish priest, who was on the platform at the time, wasn't too impressed and it was his last appearance at such a rally.

Fianna Fail, as it turned out, with the help of Labour, took over power that year. The following year, in '33, De Valera called a snap election and got an overall majority. Some years earlier, when Fianna Fail were starting out, Joe Kissane and my aunt, Mollie Maguire, had greeted De Valera on his first trip to Graignamanagh. Dev had been my aunt's maths teacher when she was studying in Carysfort Teacher Training College in Dublin.

2 | THOMASTOWN, KILKENNY AND KNOCKBEG

When I had completed my education at the national school it was decided that I would attend the CBS Secondary school in Kilkenny as there were no secondary schools in Graignamanagh. It meant that I would move to Thomastown and live with my uncle John, my aunt Nan and their family, no questions asked. Naturally this was a big break and I was very sad leaving my family in Graignamanagh. From there I could join the Waterford train up to Kilkenny, so for two years I would commute everyday from Thomastown to the CBS secondary school in Kilkenny.

My uncle and aunt lived in Noreview Terrace, a terrace of three houses in the grounds of St. Columbas nursing home. Uncle John was a house painter, like my father, and my aunt Nan was a nurse. They had eight children, three girls and five boys. Their eldest son, Phil, was a priest, another, Paddy, was an officer in the army. Two other sons, Jimmy and Henry, were painters with their father, and they, believe it or not, had the contract to paint the famous Mount Juliet. During my stay there, I had the privilege of visiting the house and estate on occasion. All three girls, Mary Margaret, Kathleen and Chrissy, attended the Presentation Convent school in Kilkenny, opposite the CBS, travelling to it each day by train also.

Starting in the CBS in Kilkenny was daunting at first as I was a stranger and knew nobody but soon I had a couple of other lads from Thomastown and Ballyhale for company. Within a few weeks of beginning school I was moved from first year to third year, mainly I believe, because of my fluency in Irish. The principal was a Brother Byrne, Brother Kiely I recall, taught Irish, French and trained the hurling team and a Mr Bolger taught maths.

Each day I would walk, with my school-bag which contained a flask of cocoa and sandwiches, from the house to the station in Thomastown, and then from the station in Kilkenny to the school on James Street, and back again in the evening, I don't ever remember getting wet, but sure I must have got wet sometime!

We had a routine each lunch time where a few of us would walk down as far as the Parade beside the Castle. On occasion we would see Mick Loughman, a postman who was also involved with the hurling team, watching to see whether any of the lads were smoking.

Every day after school, those of us waiting for the train back to Thomastown and Ballyhale had time to do our homework. Peter McBride from Ballyhale, Liam Long, Phil Hanrahan, the two McConville brothers, Tadgh Fleming who was the son of the Thomastown station master would gather in a school room. Jimmy Langton, who was also one of the group, didn't catch the train but lived out the country in a place called Lavistown. I was a great admirer of Jimmys, he was a fantastic hurler and would later become a famous Kilkenny player. He had, however, very little interest in academics so I would often help him with his French and Irish if he needed it.

Every Wednesday afternoon we had hurling practice in St James Park. We were out this day training with Brother Kiely and Mick Loughman, and Kiely said to me 'I notice Langton's Irish has improved considerably since you came around the place, but don't try it on with maths!. In the end I wasn't good enough to make the college team, but it was great thrill nevertheless when we won the Colleges All Ireland final in 1936, with Jimmy Langton leading the team. Another memorable occasion I recall was when we were given a half-day from school to go out and see 'Cobhams Air Circus', an airshow displaying the latest planes. A group of us walked a good bit outside of the town to see the aerobatics which were great as it was the first time any of us had got near a plane.

I remember one unfortunate stormy night, Brother Byrne, who was a good man, and Mr Bolger, the maths teacher who wasn't considered as good because of his frequent use of the leather, were out for a walk when they heard this unmerciful crack. They quickly separated with one going one way and the other going the opposite way, but sadly Brother Byrne was killed. A tree had fallen on him, blown down by the storm. Brother Coffey took over as principal after that and proved as wizened and contrary as a man could get. He had no interest in hurling whatsoever and we ended up giving him the nickname 'Tom God', we'd say 'here's Tom God comin!'

There was school on Saturdays back then, but as nobody in my uncle's house got up early on a Saturday morning, I was able to lie in too. Those Saturdays were mainly spent in the fields and hills near the house. Having access to the fields surrounding the St. Columbas' nursing home proved advantageous as my cousin Jimmy was able to teach me how to ride his motor bike and my cousin Paddy, how to shoot, using mainly rabbits as the targets. These skills would, later on, prove helpful when I would join the army and its motor squadron.

Even though my uncle and aunt were very kind to me during my stay in Thomastown, I remember it was lonely at times. Here was a boy who was used to going home to his family every day, and playing with his friends in the evening time, who was now living with three girls, and boys who were much older than him, in a town in which he knew very few. This experience of being away from home, however, almost certainly held me in good stead for my time at Knockbeg College which was to follow.

Knockbeg College

I achieved a good result in my Inter Cert, but a note attached to the results said I might have done better if I had attended school on Saturdays. Naturally there was a conference held, decisions had to be made. The decision was the C.B.S. was out and I would attend Knockbeg College. This decision would also have been influenced by my aunt Mollie, who was a great supporter of the Irish language. Aunt Mollie would have been aware of Knockbeg's reputation as a minor seminary that promoted the Irish language. Also, there would have been a number of students from Graignamanagh attending, so that's where I ended up. Aunt Mollie had never married and was a religious person who may have thought I had a vocation for the priesthood. I know that she helped in a big way with my college fees and would help me again years later when she would buy me my first motor car.

Knockbeg College was situated on its own grounds, three miles outside of Carlow, next to the River Barrow and was a well-known boarding school at the time. By the time I started there the school term was already well under way. The college had many dormitories that were full, but because I was senior I was assigned to a comfortable, six-bed spare room. I fitted in quite well but there was one particular guy, Ted Laffey was his name, who sat behind me in the study, and who would repeatedly hit me on the back. Having had enough one day, I said to him 'if you hit me again you'll get one back!'. Some other evening he hit me again, and true to my word he got 'one back'. This resulted in a trip to the 'boot hall' to finish what he started where he soon discovered he was no match for me. That was the last time he bothered me.

Knockbeg College.

The teachers in Knockbeg were mainly lay teachers. We had a Mr. Mc Parland and Tommy Butler, a lovely hurler, from 'The Rower' outside Graignamanagh, on the River Barrow. Butlers of the Rower was a pub that was burned down by the Black n' Tans during the Tan war. There was a Mr. Manning who taught languages and then there was a Seosamh O'Connacháin. O'Connacháin was teaching us English. He had fought for Franco out in Spain and they had fixed him up with a job when he came back. His brother, Gearoid O'Connacháin, was a founder of Altira na hAiseighe – Soldiers of the Resurrection – a short-lived Republican movement.

Irish was spoken at all times in Knockbeg, which was no problem to me, but Latin being a compulsory subject proved problematic as I hadn't studied it in the C.B.S. Because I was weak at Latin, Mr. Manning, the language teacher, would jokingly refer to me as "An Barbarach!" (the barbarian). Personally I had little interest in Latin, but as Knockbeg was a minor seminary it was part of the curriculum.

There were many young seminarians in Knockbeg and students were constantly being pushed by the rector to consider the priesthood. I never felt I had a 'calling', however when I would go up to get the results of my monthly exams the rector he would always ask, 'An bhuil tu ag caoineamh ar an Sagartoireach?' 'Bím', I would respond. 'Maith a bhuachaill, he'd say, abair na paidreacha'. It was common knowledge that playing along simply meant an easier passage through the system.

I loved Irish, and enjoyed the exercises where we were instructed to take and read a sizeable book out of the library and compose an Irish synopsis of it. That's how my Irish became so good. One book that I recall working on was titled 'She, the Transmigration of Souls'. When Mr. Manning saw me struggling with this he said 'where did you get that ?' I replied 'it was in the library'. He then informed me that it was on the banned list and I was not permitted to continue the translation. Everything was taught through Irish in Knockbeg, even subjects like geology, with its complicated scientific terminology, so over time my vocabulary must have been better in Irish than it was in English.

The accommodation in Knockbeg was comfortable and warm but the food was not very appetizing or adequate. We were accommodated in spare rooms, and we soon discovered that our predecessors had lifted a floor board in our room providing access to a space underneath to keep a biscuit tin, perfect for hiding 'prog'.

There was a tuck shop run by the college where you could buy sweets and was very handy when you had a few bob. In the winter afternoons, particularly on Sundays, the rector would run a 'whist' drive, and we won prizes on occasion. I remember winning a prize, I can't remember whether it was 15 or 30 shillings, but it was a large amount those days. The rector doled it out to me in small amounts because there was a suspicion that senior students would take drink when out at games. I welcomed the few bob though and paid a couple of visits, naturally, to the tuck shop. I remember two fairly good sized bars of chocolate I would buy called Hikers Joy and Half Time Jimmy. They were made by Urney, an Irish company no longer in existence. An tAthair Peadar was a Fior Gael and would support home industry by selling Irish produce in the tuck shop.

At that time there was a bakery in Graignamanagh, O'Leary's bakery, it delivered to the college now and then. The van brought bread and confectionaries, as well as bringing parcels from home, to students whose families lived in and near Graignamanagh. There was a rule that if you received a parcel of food from home you had to hand it up to the nun in the kitchen for general distribution. Naturally we were anxious to hold onto our prog so one day myself and my friend, John Hughes, who knew the driver, were chosen to intercept the parcels directly from the van to prevent them ending up in the refectory. We slipped out just as the van was arriving and picked up the parcels even having sufficient time to purchase some additional 'Mollie' cakes for the biscuit tin. On our way back however, we were intercepted by Fr. P.A. Maher who summarily frog marched us to the kitchen and ordered us to hand over the goodies to the nun. There was considerable consternation when we returned empty-handed, so after a bit of a conference John Hughes and myself agreed to go back and talk with the nun in an effort to retrieve some of the supplies.

Up we went to the nun and talked to her for a bit, chatting about our families, where we lived and so on. Eventually feeling sorry for us, we started getting a few things back from the nun. Unaware of our success, the other boys had decided we were taking too long so they quietly crept into the kitchen from the rear and helped themselves to the lion's share of the goodies! That was alright but a night or two later, while we were in the study, Fr. Maher, a tall, pompous kind of a man, came along and put a charge sheet down beside myself and Hughes. A real legal looking document, it listed a string of offences we were deemed to have committed including breaking the rule of bounds and so on. We had a dean of discipline at that time, Fr. R.V. Powell was his name, and it was he who had to deliver the punishment and sign the charge sheets. We'd often get notes for him but instead of going up to get the punishment we'd forge R.v. Powell on it and hand it back up again. This time however, we thought it was too serious a charge and so we decided we'd have to face the music. We knocked on the door. "Come in", said Father Powell. We stepped inside and handed him the charge sheets. We could see a smile coming on his face as he read through the charges. 'Is it possible ye lads are not able to get the parcels in without getting caught?' 'Don't get caught again' he said, signing the sheet and handing it back to us. We were beside ourselves with relief as we walked back down the corridor.

However, because we had been caught we were now liable to be searched at any time and some of us became the subjects for regular search. The occasional Oxo box with a ration of butter was the only find as we had taken the necessary precautions to avoid detection as suggested by R.V. Powell. I recall the rector pulling me up one day and catching me with some contraband. 'Buachaill naireach drochbhronach i gconai ag teacht amach as na conai' he called referring to me as a 'bold, bad mannered boy, always coming out of corners!'

A priest had been sent around from Rome at that time, to visit all the minor seminaries on inspection. The rector picked two students from each class to be interviewed. Our class wasn't happy with his choice so John Hughes and myself were asked to represent them instead. We visited the priest and made our complaints. Food was number one on our list. We also made a big issue about the subjects included in the curriculum, making particular reference to languages. The priest was friendly and took our complaints onboard without comment. The rector became aware of the switch and soon after, a group of us including John Hughes and myself were wrongly accused of damaging a piece of furniture during some horse play in a hallway. We were not involved but we were still summoned to the office of the dean of discipline, Fr. Maher. Once he started in with the leather strap, the two other lads immediately began to cry, but I refused so he continued with me until I eventually gave in. It left me in a bad way and going into the oratory that night to say prayers I was shaking all over.

Many years later, in the 1950s, travelling by train from Dublin to

Dundalk, I recognised a priest sitting opposite me in the carriage. It was Fr. Ryan, the same priest who had visited our minor seminary all those years ago and listened to our complaints. We had a great chat and Fr. Ryan acknowledged that our complaints at the time were valid but that they couldn't admit it.

Most of the teachers were good crack though, including Mr. Mc Parland, the maths teacher. He was a brilliant man but a poor teacher. There was a fellow in our class called Joe Bannon, a lazy character who never bothered much with work and was always yawning and stretching. This day during a lesson, reclining in his seat at the back of the class, Bannon stretched out and had a big yawn. Mc Parland, seeing this, let fly with the chalk and got him straight in his mouth. Bannon was never able to live that one down.

During the summer most Sunday afternoons were used for organised activities. There were gaps though and those of us who were swimmers could not resist the call of the river Barrow. We went swimming in the river which was the boundary between the counties of Carlow and Laois. Our favourite spot was near the canal lock where we could swim and also enjoy the rough water over the weir. Mr. Watchhorn, the lock-keeper, was usually nearby.

One Sunday a few of us went to the River and got a lift to the Carlow side. We walked along the river bank into the town where we enjoyed a meal of bangers and mash at the Castle Cafe. Our absence was not noticed. Our luck had held and so we enjoyed a few similar trips. The rector, An t'athair Peadar never knew.

The great Tommy Murphy "The Boy Wonder"

Tommy Murphy was a day boy at Knockbeg and his father the steward over the diocesan property on the surrounding land. A great footballer, he played at senior level for Co Laois and for Knockbeg. He played a little hurling and had agreed to play hurling for the school. We had no recognised trainer at the time and I recall the rector taking the hurling squad out to his home village in Ballon, Co Carlow one Sunday, to play the local camogie team, which was an experience. Tommy was a very fit athlete and his long arms allowed him to catch the sliothar over our heads but he didn't have the necessary experience in handling the hurley and so would often 'kick' the sliotar over the bar rather than hit it. In Gaelic, he would later earn the title "The Boy Wonder" for his displays in both the senior ranks on the national scene and as a college student but never won an All-Ireland medal. His ability, however, would be recognised, years later, by his inclusion in the Millenium team and he appeared on a 30c stamp, issued by An Post, to mark that special occasion.

During my second year in Knockbeg, I was playing well enough to be selected for the senior college team, and lined up alongside the famous Tommy Murphy in the Leinster Colleges championship where we played the Kilkenny C.B.S. in Dr Cullen Park. Tommy was scheduled to play Gaelic for Laois against Kerry later that afternoon and so he would only be available to play for us for the first half of the game.

On the morning of the match, after breakfast, we were supposed to go and say a prayer in the oratory but we decided not to go up this day. Taking a shortcut instead to avoid the prayers, I managed to hit my toe off a step while running down and found myself barely able to walk. The lads wouldn't let me go to the infirmary as they knew that once the nurse saw my injury I wouldn't be allowed to play, and I had to play as I could generally be relied upon to get a score.

It was decided to cut the toe out of my football boot to relieve the pressure. As we were waiting for our lift into Dr Cullen Park, the rector, an t'Athair Peadar, came over and told four of us big lads to walk the four miles to Carlow. He had been ferrying the lads into town for the match but obviously wanted to save himself an extra journey. During the first half of the game Tommy kicked a point to everybody's delight. I had been instructed to stay on the corner of the square during the game, that way I'd get a score, which I did but it was disallowed. The official maintained I was in the square when in fact I wasn't. Sadly, we were beaten by a point. If only my goal hadn't been disallowed we'd have been in the semi-final of the Leinster Colleges championship.

Certificate of Service.

3 | THE EMERGENCY AND THE ARMY

During the summer of 1940 we were on holidays from school awaiting the results of the Leaving Cert, and occupied those long summer days by swimming, fishing and picnicking. Occasionally we would gather frauchains (bilberries) on the slopes of Brandon Hill and in the nearby woods to sell locally and earn some pocket money.

The Kilkenny hurling team was playing well, heading for a two in a row having won the 'thunder and lightning' final the previous year, interestingly on the same day that war was declared, Limerick beat them 3-7 to 1-7 in 1940.

Naturally we followed the progress of the war with enthusiasm. We were limited however, with what we learned from the papers as they were subject to censorship. We got most of our news about the outside world and even Ireland via the battery-operated wireless. There was a strong feeling of national pride amongst everyone at the time and Lord Haw Haw's radio show, which had a wide listening audience, was very popular. His endless taunting of the British Establishment was highly entertaining. Haw Haw's famous or infamous taunt however, that he could speak better English than the stuttering king or bow-legged queen enraged the English people and most certainly helped sign his death warrant in the end. Rationing was also very strict and items like tea were in strong demand. Songs like 'Bless De Valera and Sean Mc Entee, they gave us the brown bread and a half ounce of tea' only served to strengthen our national sentiment.

When the war started in 1939 Mr. De Valera declared neutrality and he was backed up by the leaders of the other political parties like Mr. W.T. Cosgrove, Fine Gael, and Mr. William Norton, the leader of the Labour party. There was one exception in the Dail from Cumann na Gael, one James Dillon. He called on the Irish people to join with England and defeat Hitler's army. The feeling amongst us all at that time was, sure we had never fought against anybody only England so why now, should we go fight against Germany? All of our political leaders were united in their call to the young people of Ireland, "Join the Defence Forces and defend our country". Our national pride was at an all-time high so when this call to volunteer came we didn't hesitate. A whole lot of us went down to the local Garda Barracks in Graignamanagh and gave our names to the sergeant in charge, Sgt. Doyle, I can remember him well. Sometime afterwards only myself and my friend Liam Doyle, were called up by the recruiting officer, Captain Martin Bates. He administered the oath and swore us in. We were then driven, in the back of his nice saloon car, to Kilkenny Military Barracks where we arrived at about lunch time, and were handed over to the duty officer. It was dinner time so we were taken to the dining hall for our first army meal where we had to borrow utensils and wash them in a bucket of water at the dining hall door.

The water would have started off very hot and clean but as it had been used repeatedly by the previous diners before we got there it was now greasy and cold. With the dinner piled on our plates we sat down opposite each other. A fist full of salt squatted amidst the potato peels and other debris strewn over the timber table. Not a very appetizing sight even for two people who were used to the frugal fare at Knockbeg College. Liam looked over at me and said 'Are you thinking the same as I'm thinking? If only I hadn't taken the oath, I'd be out that door fast!'

After we had finished eating our initial disappointment soon gave way to a sense of adventure as we joined a group of recruits en route to the Curragh Camp. We arrived by truck at Connolly Barracks sometime in the evening and were treated to our tea which consisted of a ration of bread, a quarter of a loaf with some butter and a mug of tea. Connolly Barracks would be home for the next two months as we were taken through our induction and basic training. I was now Private James O'Shea No. 80788 and Liam was No. 80786, some fella had gotten in between the two of us.

I was issued with a new uniform which consisted of a grey shirt, tunic, trousers, socks, heavy boots, short leggings and a cap. I also received dog tags, my pay book in which I would record my weekly pay, 13-2 a week, and a 'housewife', pronounced 'Hussive', which was a pouch that contained needles and thread so we could darn holes in our socks and stitch on buttons when required. Most importantly I was issued with my very own 303 Lee Enfield rifle and was instructed by the quartermaster to guard it with my life and treat it as my new best friend as I might need it later on.

Our company sergeant then gave us three words of wisdom to adhere to, to avoid getting into trouble in the army; cleanliness, obedience and punctuality, so you kept yourself clean, you were on time and you did what you were told.

Manning the Vickers machine gun,

water tower, Curragh 1940.

After a while we gradually became accustomed to the daily routine of marching out on the square, square bashing as it was called, and rifle drill. We got the impression that we were being used to steamroll the barracks square. With that amount of square bashing I was lucky to escape getting blisters on my feet which lots of the others got due to the heavy boots. Reveille would sound at 7a.m. each morning after which you got dressed and answered a roll call. Breakfast then followed and when finished we'd return to our billet to stand beside our bed, which would then be inspected to check that everything was clean and tidy. One member of the billet would be nominated as room orderly for the day and was responsible for keeping the billet tidy, including scrubbing the floor when necessary. Following this we went out to the square to do foot-drill, jogging and running - the foundations of commando training.

After a few days I received notification to attend an interview for an officers' course. The interview board was made up of a number of officers and chaired by Colonel McNally, the O.C.

of The Curragh command. I was asked various questions by the board, my life before the army, schooling, what games I played etc. During the course of the interview I stupidly asked the question 'how can I become an officer when I don't know anything about soldiering ?' Colonel McNally replied 'Well if that's the way you feel, ok, you go out and do your soldiering and then apply for the officers' course, I left the interview knowing that I had talked my way out of a shortcut to the officer grade.

When the initial training was done in Connolly Barracks I was posted to the motorized Cavalry Corps in McDermott Barracks. I was no sooner down there when Quartermaster Sergeant Fouvarge, who was of French extraction, grabbed me and assigned me office duties. He had seen I had my Leaving Cert and he wanted someone reliable to work for him. I was happy as could be down there having various military duties to perform as well as general office work. One of these duties was manning, as part of a team, a Vickers machine gun on the roof of the water tower nearby.

I got on well with the CQM and learned much from him particularly his typical army language which I disliked at first but eventually became used to. Christmas was approaching and Sergeant Fouvarge had promised to arrange leave for me to get home for Christmas but other events were to intervene.

My First Christmas away from Home

There were two canteens in the Curragh, one situated beside us at McDermott Barracks called the Wesley Home and another, which was away at the other end of the camp, called the Sand's Soldiers Home. This particular day a few of us were in the Wesley Home having a cup of tea when we noticed smoke rising from the IRA internment camp down at Tin Town. Seconds later, the general alarm went off and the military police arrived to order us back to our units.

When we got back to our units we found out that the IRA, in their protests, had set fire to some of the huts in the internment camp. This had exposed an escape tunnel which was almost complete. Apparently there had been a split in the IRA camp and one crowd didn't know what the other was doing. By burning the huts down they had inadvertently revealed the near complete tunnel and foiled their own escape plot. A foggy night was all that was needed to facilitate the escape of the entire camp.

Because of the incident everything was tightened up in the camp and all Christmas leave was cancelled. This was hugely disappointing so we decided to celebrate Christmas with a get-together in the Sands Soldiers Home instead. Sand's Soldiers Home stood as a relic of the British days in The Curragh. It was run by a group of genteel old world Protestant ladies and was very popular with the other ranks. The social life in the Curragh was minimal. Sand's Soldiers Home offered tea, had a selection of pastries available and had a cinema attached, so was an important feature in the camp.

Soldiers were paid 13/2 a week but married men had 7/- deducted and sent home to their wives. Pay day was on a Wednesday so by the weekend money was scarce. One Sunday morning a few men from nearby Plunkett Barracks were attracted to music coming from Sand's Home and went to investigate. They entered through the open door and joined in the singing of some hymns. On conclusion of the singing the lads were invited to have some refreshments. They gladly accepted. This source of goodies was kept a secret by the recipients who continued to visit for a few Sundays. Eventually the chaplain, Fr Casey, heard of the event and made it the subject of his Sunday homily accusing the lads of taking part in Protestant worship which was a reserved sin at one time. The lecture had the opposite effect however, the secret was now out, and there was an increase in numbers attending which contributed to the early end of this accidental ecumenical gathering.

On Christmas day, as planned, all the lads from Graignamanagh went down to Sand's Home to celebrate and have a bit of grub and we began lamenting the fact we were not at home eating with our families instead. We were unaware that arrangements for Christmas dinner had been put in place for us back at the dining hall. Sometime later, after we had finished stuffing ourselves with Chester cake, we returned to our barracks to be greeted by a full Christmas dinner that had been laid on for us, white table cloths included, by the officers who supervised distribution of the food. Barely able to start the dinner let alone finish it, we struggled to do the meal justice but gave it our best attempt.

The Fifth Motor Squadron

Christmas was over and things had settled down. I was in the quartermasters office performing my usual duties when the door opened and in walked Colonel McNally. 'What were you told to do? Weren't you told to get out and do your proper training. You're not going to do it sitting on your tail end in here in an office'. 'There's a course on at the moment, get out and get on it,' he told me, referring to a course that was about to begin which would allow me to train as a corporal.

So I did the course and received my first stripe, and I was posted to the 5th Motor Squadron as part of the Fifth Brigade. So here I was, a young corporal going into a completely new unit. The Fifth Motor Squadron had just been formed at the time under Comdt Johnny Stapleton and his second in command, Capt Timmy Ryan, who were both inspiring figures. Everybody was new going into the unit and it was an exciting place as it meant driving various motor vehicles including BSA 500cc motor cycles. It had five troops in it, including an armoured car troop as well. The main armament would be rifle, revolver and the Bren gun, which was a light automatic machine gun. Armoured cars would have the big heavy Vickers machine guns mounted in their turrets. We were required to complete additional training for this new unit, in particular advanced motorcycling training. Courses were run by Sergeant Brennan, or battle-axe Brennan as he was known. The director of training was Stanley Woods who had won the Isle of Man T.T. We were taught simple daily maintenance and important things like how to rough-ride our bikes across country and fall from the motorcycle properly. Donnelly's Hollow, a famous place outside of the Curragh named after the renowned bare fist pugilist, Dan Donnelly 1788-1820, was frequently used as a location for our motor cycle training. For me, this was a much more exciting place to be rather than stuck in an office somewhere, and I finally felt that I was doing what I had signed up to do.

The Fifth Motor Squadron was billeted in Tintown beside the I.R.A. internment camp and was close to Plunkett Barracks at the west end of the Curragh camp. Security was paramount so each unit was well separated from the next with heavy stakes and barbed wire covered by raised sentry boxes. We were also quite close to the 'Glass house', a jail for the defaulters in the army. Internment camps next to us were made up of tin sheds, and big stoves in the middle for burning turf, if you could get the turf to burn. Next to the IRA internees were the German internees, some of whom were German survivors rescued by the M.V. *Kerlogue*, an Irish vessel which had picked them up after their ship was sunk off the Irish coast. They had great marching tunes and some mornings on their way to the baths they could be heard singing at the top of their voices. These Germans eventually got parole and some would go to work for Bord na Mona cutting turf.

At this time the spirit in the army was tremendous. Even though we had limited equipment, what we had we could use with effect, and our training was of the highest calibre. Before I left the Curragh I could swim the length of the swimming pool in full battle dress, with a steel helmet and a rifle over my shoulder. I had also proudly achieved a chevron as marksman for both the rifle and the Bren gun. Because our squadron was now fully functional we were expecting a move and rumours were rife as to where we were going. We soon learned that we were being sent to Kilkenny castle.

Return to Kilkenny

I received orders from my commanding officer to take my section of the squadron to Kilkenny castle as an advance party and provide some military presence in the castle yard, which was across the road from the castle itself. Kilkenny castle was the headquarters of the Fifth Brigade, which included infantry, artillery, cavalry and signals, it was an entire fighting unit.

I assembled my lads together, prepared the equipment and drove down to Kilkenny where I made contact with the Office of Public Works. We then secured the castle yard and awaited the arrival of the rest of the squadron. Eventually the main body arrived and we began adjusting to our new surroundings. Firstly we began to familiarize ourselves with the local area by patrolling around Kilkenny, down to Waterford and also Wexford. Our primary function would be to protect the southern part of the country if there was an invasion and so local knowledge of the south coast was essential. We conducted regular mounted patrols and military exercises all over the region.

These frequent operations meant that daily maintenance of the vehicles and proper fuel management was essential. The way we used to fill the vehicles with petrol, petrol would be stored in 50-gallon drums and we'd have them up on a trestle. Petrol would be drawn off from the larger drums into smaller two gallon metal containers, which were in common use at the time, and then poured into the vehicles. At times some vehicles didn't take the full two gallons and what was left would be poured back into the 50-gallon drum, but it was always recorded as two nevertheless. The result was over time we accumulated a fuel surplus. This presented a bit of a problem as there had been some pilfering in the military barracks at that time and a surplus of petrol might tempt pilferers. During an inspection the surplus was noted by the commanding officer. Annoyed, the officer asked, 'Now that my attention has been drawn to this, what are we going to do with it ?. 'We have men who need extra training' I suggested, 'and there are some vehicles with broken speedometers. If we fill those vehicles with the surplus and use them to train the men it would be the easiest and safest way to do it'. Agreeing, the officer ordered that, in future, accurate fuel consumption records be kept to ensure that the surplus did not occur again. It was a point in my favour.

Comdt. Mackey, who was an intelligence officer from headquarters, came to inspect all the bridges in south Kilkenny, Waterford and Wexford, to ensure they were prepared for demolition in the event of an invasion. My section was assigned to accompany him as we made our way to each location. We got along well and I recall we had fine weather for the duration and enjoyed it immensely. When we returned Comdt. Mackey complimented me to my commanding officer, Johnny Stapleton, stating 'He knows his map reading !, Soon after a vacancy

33

occurred for sergeant and I was promoted.

Paddy Summers, Jim O' Shea
Castle Yard, Kilkenny 1942.

We were out on manoeuvres, scattered all over the place with each unit in a different location, some in Carlow and others in Kilkenny. As a sergeant I was with one group down around New Ross. The O.C. came to me and said 'On your way back, would you call round and say hello to your mother', instructing me to visit her on my way back to Kilkenny. I was wondering what he meant. Apparently a section of the squadron had arrived in Graignamanagh and happened to stop outside my family home. My mother, being a friendly woman, had come out and offered the lads a cup of tea. When they told the O.C. that the woman had given them tea, he went over to thank her. She replied that she was simply doing what she would like someone else to do for her own son in similar circumstances. 'Why, have you a son in the army?' the officer asked. 'I have' she responded. 'What's his name?' he asked. 'O'Shea, he's in the Fifth Motor Squadron'. 'Sure this is the Fifth Motor Squadron !' he replied.

An hour later I pulled up outside our house on my BSA 500. My mother hadn't seen me in my uniform before so this was a big occasion for her especially when the neighbours came out to see what all the commotion was about. I was wondering, afterwards, where she got the tea to give to the soldiers, as tea was a rare commodity back then. She must have had a secret stash put away for special occasions.

The 1942 Manoeuvres

In August of 1942 the Fifth Motor Squadron as part of Second Division, took part in one of the biggest army manoeuvres ever undertaken in the state. The First Division, based in Cork under the command of Col. Mickey Joe Costello, a well known character in army circles at the time, was the invading group and Second Division, commanded by Col. McNeil, were sent down south to intercept and repel the invading force. We engaged in a number of exercises as we moved into strategic areas of importance in south Tipperary like Ara Glen for example. We would set up positions to acquire specific targets and afterward make further advances. It was also an endurance test for both divisions as, during one exercise, there was no provision for food or sleep for a 72-hour period. This took its toll on the men with at least one recorded fatality, a drowning in the Blackwater. The manoeuvres went on for some time and ended with a big parade of the participating troops who marched through Cork city. After cleaning some of the vehicles in a local stream, which had been muddied over the course of the manoeuvres, we joined the parade. Mr. De Valera was there, and he took the salute from the troops as we passed by.

On our way back it was decided we'd go as far as Youghal, to take a break and get a few days rest before we returned to Kilkenny Castle. The town was well prepared and the publicans in Youghal were given an extra supply of alcohol to cope with the influx of troops. After a few days our plans changed because of a confrontation between the pubs and some troops over drink not being available. Luckily our squadron was not involved in the incident and to retain our good name our O.C. decided to return to barracks, so we headed back to Kilkenny.

Back to the Curragh

We resumed our normal routine in Kilkenny and were soon into '43. In the new year I was informed by the O.C. that there was an officer's course starting at the Curragh. I said 'I don't think I'll bother'. The O.C. replied 'I knew you'd say that, you're for interview at the Curragh in the morning', ordering me to attend the interview the next day. He also instructed me to visit the tailor in the Cavalry Depot and get my uniform pressed beforehand to be presentable. I attended the interview and was accepted so I found myself back at the Curragh, again, on a provisional officers' course at Connolly Barracks.

On completion of the course we moved to the Military College, which was run by Colonel Gallagher, to continue our training. Col. Gallagher spoke to us in clear language explaining what we could expect during our training. Battle dress would be worn regularly and we would be required to always run when outdoors. Comdt. Charlie McGoohan would be in charge of training. Discipline would be strict and he and his instructors ensured the regime was enforced at all times. Any participant caught defaulting would be severely punished. A real military man, when McGoohan trained you, you stayed trained! Amongst those training with us at Pearse Barracks were Douglas Gageby, who later became editor of the Irish Times, Ned Doyle, who would become a colonel and director of signals, and Simon Duignan, who won an all Ireland football final for Cavan. Liam Doyle, my childhood friend from Graignamanagh, was also on the course. One thing out of the ordinary I recall during the training was when they took us down to an abattoir and demonstrated how to indentify 'contract specification' meat, should you find yourself in an outpost somewhere and purchasing for a small unit. The main test was for T.B.

Eventually we were coming near the end of the course and myself and another trainee were selected by Comdt Thompson to visit Dame Street in Dublin where they made the uniforms. Here we were measured to provide a standard uniform size for the new officers. We also underwent a strict medical exam including X-ray.

The night before we were commissioned the director of the

Military College, Colonel Gallagher, who was an aloof kind of a person, asked each of us individually, if and when we were commissioned, where we would like to be stationed. I expressed a preference for a cavalry unit seeing as I had spent some time in it. He didn't say anymore and the following morning we attended the commissioning ceremonies which took place on the square. Here we swore an oath, 'to be faithful to Ireland and loyal to the constitution' and each received our commissions from the Minister for Defence. When we left, as lieutenants we got our first salute from the sergeant major. When the ceremony was over there were some celebrations and refreshments after which, to my surprise, I was informed that I was being posted to the 24th Battalion based at Ceannt Barracks in the Curragh.

Receiving my commission from Oscar Traynor,
Minister for Defence
Sept 1943.

My first introduction to the 24th battalion was when I arrived and the orderly officer welcomed me and brought me over to the officer's mess. When we got there he asked me 'what will you have to drink ?' I replied 'get me a lemonade' which surprised him judging from the reaction on his face. Introduced all around I met the notable Lieutenant Jack McQuillan as well as a regular officer called Tom Hartigan whom I ended up sharing a room and becoming good friends with.

My commanding officer was Major Charlie Doherty who was very active in Donegal during the War of Independence as was his brother Barney. He commandeered a vehicle for use in an operation which was sung about after, 'you can hear the din going through Glenfin in Johnsons motorcar'. Charlie lived outside the camp and would cycle to work every morning. Some mornings he would be in bad form and it was advisable to avoid him on such a morning. McQuillan, who could be very irreverent, described him on a bad morning with 'a face like an ass eating a thistle'. My company commander was Capt. Brian McGuirk whose family had to leave Belfast during the pogroms of the 1920s. He was a fine officer whom we all looked up to.

I was one of four platoon commanders in A company. We were pleased to have Lieutenant Jack McQuillan amongst us to share our duties. He was a bit of a celebrity as he had won an All-Ireland football medal in 1943 when he played with the victorious Roscommon team.

Privates were exchanged amongst the platoons and attracted the required reports from the commanders. I received Private Ryan, a native of Co Wexford, from Jack's platoon. Jack said he was 'clumsy' and described him as 'once seen never forgotten'. Apparently Private Ryan had failed rifle drill in all three platoons. On close examination I realised that he could not close his left eye while taking aim. This problem was resolved by the provision of an eye patch for the offending eye and soon after he passed rifle drill. He could not, however, shed the 'ungainly' tag. We had an influx of recruits into the battalion at that time and along with Corporal Harold O'Sullivan, I was delegated as training officer to this new group. The 24th battalion, however, being a garrison battalion, was also responsible for most protection duties in the camp. One of the most important duties was the

24-hour guard with an officer in charge, on the internment camp at Tintown. This duty was taken very seriously and entailed first being issued with ammunition, before marching down to the camp to relieve the guard on duty. It was a twenty-four hour guard broken only by the occasional nap, if you were lucky. I would be excused guard duty however, while on training duties. Corporal Harold O'Sullivan became an officer and years later we met in our new careers. Bord na Mona on lanesboro and local government in Dundalk

The Curragh had regular race meetings and we got plenty of tips for the horses. Tommy Hartigan was looking forward to a two -day meeting, the first day happened to be pay day. I paid my mess bill but Tommy Hartigan didn't as he wanted to have his full month's salary available to gamble. The first day we were cleaned out. This was tragic for Tommy as it was a very serious offence to default in paying your mess bill. After the last race we met a namesake of Tommy's who told us to meet him after the first race the following day and to bring plenty of money. I went down to the Post Office and withdrew the maximum allowed - 30 shillings. The information given to us by Tommy's friend was good as we got three nice winners and ended up making a decent profit. It proved a salutary lesson especially for Tommy with regard to his mess bill.

Officers could be detailed for duty outside the camp. A few came my way. When called out, the fire brigade was usually in the charge of an officer from the engineer corps but there was provision to have an infantry officer take his place should the need arise. One night I had to take the brigade down to Kildare golf club to deal with a fire. It had not developed so it was soon under control. Thankfully there were no injuries or major damage so the report was quite simple, the main feature of which was the particulars of the insurance company.

No 3 Army Band was stationed at the Curragh with Lieutenant Dermot O'Hara. One Sunday during the summer the band was due to attend at Clongowes Wood College for Re union Day. Dermot was not available for some reason and I was delegated to accompany the band. It was a beautiful day and the band played a lovely selection of airs and did us proud. I remember being seated at the top table for a sumptuous meal before returning to the camp.

When carrying out exercises away from the Curragh Camp we went cross country. Sometimes damage was done to fences and gates and occasionally a farmer would make a claim against the army. Captain Mickie Hanahoe, a legal officer, would investigate the claim taking me with him at times to verify we had been on the property.

The Glen of Imaal

In August of '44 our battalion moved lock, stock, and barrel to Coolmoney, near Baltinglass, to do field exercises. We had set up camp by a stream and were performing the usual daily exercises. These manoeuvres gave Lt. Jack McQuillan the perfect opportunity to prepare for the coming All Ireland final as Roscommon were in contention once again. Part of his training was drinking big pints at night and working them off the next day across the rugged Wicklow countryside. One morning, as we moved out on exercise, Jack's platoon was in the lead with responsibility to clear any opposition encountered. Jack pleaded with me to take over from him with my platoon saying that every time his heels hit the ground the top of his head seemed to lift. I agreed and everything went as normal.

We had routine marches north toward Baldonnel airfield as the battalion was responsible for the protection of its southern perimeter. Returning from exercises one evening we discovered that the stream had overflowed, flooding the entire camp. Myself and Tommy Hartigan decided to go in to Baltinglass and have a few drinks to 'stave off' a bad cold. On our way in we got sidetracked by a special picture that was being shown in the local cinema and decided to watch it instead. We then went to a hotel in Baltinglass for tea and it was fairly late when we left to go back to the camp. On our way back, still pioneers, we passed by a farm house and because it was so late we decided to bed down for the night in the hay shed. The next morning we awoke to reveille blowing in the camp, we tidied ourselves up and made our way back.

Another night a number of officers had a party at the hotel, which was owned by Lt. Harbourn's people. On the way back to camp a small number called to Jacksons pub to have 'one for the road'. Reggie Gorman ended up unable to travel and opted to stay at the pub. The others left him to the landlady who allowed him to sleep on the floor. The next morning, still missing from the camp, an ambulance was sent in for Reggie. The landlady gave him a cure of an Advocat and white lemonade and he was brought back and confined to barracks. On returning to the Curragh weeks later, Reggie was flabbergasted when he received a bill in the post for the Advocat and white lemonade from the landlady.

The next thing that happened was the All-Ireland final came along, which was a great topic of conversation, as McQuillan was on the Roscommon team. He wasn't very popular with the hierarchy. The O.C. of Curragh Command at the time, who was a nephew of Michael Collins, Sean Collins Powell, for some reason or another didn't like McQuillan. Col. Powell was speaking to Captain John Joe Keohane, the full back on the Kerry team, before the game and told him to 'stitch it in McQuillan today'. However, the first ball that came in, McQuillan put his fist into Keohane's stomach knocking the wind out of him. His training in the Glen of Imaal had paid off as Roscommon went on to beat Kerry in the All-Ireland final, giving them two-in-a-row.

Our mess at Ceannt Barracks was used by some officers from Signal and Engineer Corps. We also had officers from headquarters. They mixed very well and played snooker and poker. There were some serious poker games at the weekends. A solicitor named Manus Noonan usually won. It was suggested that he lodged his winnings in the bank when it came to the camp on a Wednesday. Years later I saw Manus was district justice in the Dundalk area.

Lullymore Bog, Foreign Games and the Civil Service

In early summer 1944 it was time for the annual turf cutting at Lullymore Bog in Kildare. A and B Companies were given the job. A big work force, most of the members were from the west of Ireland and very much at home with the 'winged slán'. It was a pleasure to see the sods being cut from the face of the bog. All were regular in size. A section of the Construction Corps supervised by a number of officers who were nearing retirement age arrived. Its members were young delinquents who had accepted the option to join instead of spending time in jail for minor offences. It was hoped that this arrangement would solve a problem on the streets of Dublin. They were to be employed on a road construction project but did not make the effort instead choosing to make a nuisance of themselves about the place. The supervising officers were replaced by a Capt. Martín Mc Gannon who wasted no time whipping them into action and the road construction began. On completion of the turf cutting we returned to the Curragh leaving Martín and his merry men to continue with the road building. When completed he gave his name to the finished product. Years later, after demobilisation, I met Martín again at Dublin Airport and later at P.V. Doyles Hotel where he was working as security.

In November 1944, Louis Culleton organised a party for a dress dance to be held at the Gresham Hotel. Officers uniform was accepted as suitable 'dress' for such occasions. I was delighted to accept his invitation to my first dress dance. It was a big change from my usual hops at tennis clubs etc. Our party was made up of past pupils and friends of the Cistercian College in Roscrea. On entry to the ballroom we received a programme giving details of the number of dances and the tunes to be played. We were introduced and suitably seated. A blind date for some of us, the 'Paul Jones' dances facilitated changes in partners. To explain, the ladies joined hands in an outward facing circle, with the men surrounding the ladies in an inward facing circle. When the music started both circles would move sideways in opposite directions. When the music stopped the circles would also and the man would ask the girl opposite him to dance. When the night had ended it was seen as a great success and we decided to have a repeat occasion in the New Year. This took place in February, 1945 at the Metropole Ballroom and was another great night.

There was a family-run hotel on Parnel Square in Dublin, known as the Anchor Hotel. It was owned by two sisters from Graignamanagh. A few of us would use it as a B and B when in Dublin. It was later bought by a 'Matt Donnelly' who modernised it adding a lounge bar. He also owned O'Briens Hotel in Parnell Street which was around the corner. Interestingly, he would open the 'Derryhale Hotel' in Dundalk many years later.

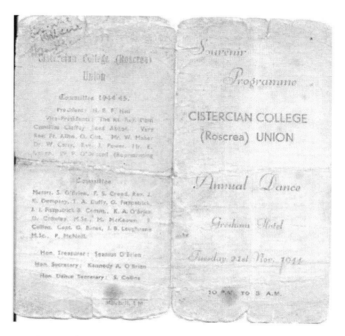

Souvenir Programme, Dress Dance 1944 (outside).

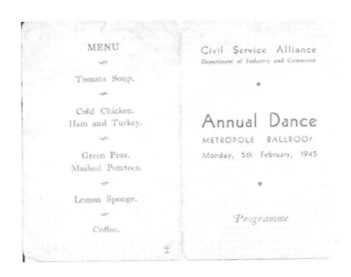

Souvenir Programme, Dress Dance 1945 (outside).

Souvenir Programme, Dress Dance 1945 (inside).

The Gresham Hotel 1944.

On the 18th March 1945, myself and Jack McQuillan were again sent with a work party from the battalion to cut turf at Lullymore. One of us would travel back to the Curragh once a week to get our rations. One day I arrived at the quarter masters office to be informed that the commanding officer wanted to see me. I went up and knocked at the door and was told to come in. When I opened the door I was met with a barrage of bad language from the O.C. 'I don't give a 'F' for Seamus Gardiner,' he said, and went on and on until finally I said 'Excuse me, but would you mind telling me what this is all about? ' 'Do you not read the Times? ' he asked me. 'And where would I get the Times in Lullymore Bog? ' I replied. He cooled down a little bit and I went back and loaded up the rations and returned to Lullymore Bog. Apparently there had been a dispute between the GAA and the Minister for Defence regarding the playing of foreign games in the army. Seamus Gardiner was the president of the GAA at the time. In an exchange of letters that had taken place, some extracts from 'general orders' of the 24th Battalion had been published in the *Times*. These extracts indicated that some members of the battalion attended a soccer match. Jack

McQuillan, having won All-Ireland medals in '43 and '44 for Roscommon, was suspected as being the provider of the information, and by association I came under suspicion. Jack and I were friendly but I did not know anything about this incident.

One day I accompanied a senior officer from Dublin selecting locations in the bog for some of the Dublin battalions, I was drenched in a shower of rain which dried on me when the sun came out. I ended up getting a cold which developed into septic tonsils leaving me in a bad way. Because of the telephone system back then, we were only connected for an hour, twice a day, to the Curragh. I remember Jack McQuillan demanding a doctor and an ambulance be sent out to take me to hospital. I was treated on the officer's ward with ground up M&B tablets, which were very hard to swallow, as there was no such thing as penicillin at the time. After spending three weeks in hospital I was released and got three weeks sick leave to go back to Graignamanagh and recuperate. There was a carnival on at the time and I won most of the prizes at the shooting range.

When I returned to my unit I was sent as an instructor to the FCA officers course in Tramore. I got word from Tadgh O' Sullivan, who was already down there, to bring a bottle or two from the mess which I duly did. 'The lovely man', Capt. O' Connell, was travelling down with me on the train, which was packed. O' Connell had a good voice and as we stood in the overcrowded corridor he began to sing. Some women from an adjacent carriage made room for us to travel down with them. 'The lovely man' broke his journey in Waterford while I crossed the quays of Waterford to the station for Tramore and continued on my way. After returning from Tramore and its training during the day and nights in the 'Atlantic Ballroom', I was sent to the RDS to take charge of a composite unit at a display known as a 'tattoo. ' This gave the army an opportunity to show the public our range of vehicles and weaponry at close range. Some of the motor squadrons gave 'dare-devil' stunts on the motor bikes. Other groups gave demonstrations in commando exercises.

The war had ended and demobilisation began and those who had temporary commissions were given the opportunity to apply for permanent positions. There were limited vacancies available however. I applied and was asked during the interview if not retained on full time would I remain on reserve, my reply to which was 'no'. When the results became known I found that I had not been accepted and often felt afterward that the dispute between the GAA and the Minister for Defence had played a part in my failure to be retained as a regular officer.

Demobilization was a phased affair. To release the entire number of soldiers in one lot would have caused havoc on the labour market. Attempts were made to prepare as many as possible for civilian life. Myself and another officer, Jack Coffey, found ourselves training soldiers how to drive. We spent months doing this, turning out competent drivers who could handle heavy lorries.

Waiting on demob 1946.

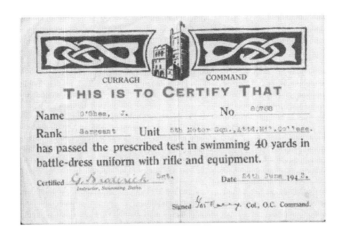

Curragh Command certificate.

A Command Headquarters
Christmas Dinner Menu,
Ceannt Barracks 1945.

Army Pay Book
1942 - 1943,
Sgt. Jim O' Shea.

First tactical course, Nov 1942 Kilkenny.

Officer Commanding and Officers 24th Infantry Battalion,
October 1945.

4 | BORD NA MONA

Before leaving the army we were given the opportunity to study for the Junior X (Junior executive) civil service exam. I didn't want the civil service and chose to do an interview for Aer Lingus instead, as I preferred the idea of working outside as opposed to being stuck in an office. The position I applied for was in ground transport at Shannon airport. After the interview I was promised the position but was informed that they would not be ready to start for several months. In the meantime they offered me a clerical job which I refused, instead waiting for the promised job, taking for granted that I had secured the position. When I called back at the end of summer I was informed that Aer Lingus had made other arrangements with CIE regarding their ground transport, and that the job was no longer available.

I then heard that they were looking for supervisors in Bord na Mona. I applied and my application was successful. In 1945 and 1946, Bord na Mona was planning for modernisation and extension. At the same time they were under severe pressure to supply turf for general consumption on the home market. Getting the workers to the bogs and the turf to the market was a big problem. The transport was not in place to cope. Sometime earlier, British and German internees at the Curragh were granted a liberal parole. Seeing this, the Bord made a special arrangement with the Dept of Defence to acquire some German internees from the Curragh to work in the Kildare bogs.

My first assignment was a period of training in Lullymore Bog, the largest single-raised-bog in the Bog of Allen, a place I was familiar with from my time in the army. My wages were six pounds per week while I was in training which would increase substantially later on. While at Lullymore I saw all the different machines in use. Most turf-cutting machines were either German or Belgian made and very impressive. During the war years however, maintenance was carried out by Thompsons of Carlow and G.N.R. Works at Dundalk. Bord engineers were constantly trying to get in contact with the German and Belgian companies but couldn't as conditions in Europe at the time were chaotic. Parts were not readily available and so the Irish firms were forced to keep the show on the road by performing the required modifications needed to adapt to Ireland's unique bogs, themselves.

The machines worked on caterpillar wheels and moved slowly along the top of the bog scooping out the turf and emptying it into the hopper. The turf was then macerated and pushed through a nozzle onto a conveyor belt, where the sods were guillotined, mechanically turned over, and spread in neat rows on top of the bog. This was known as machine-won turf, as distinct from hand-cut turf.

After Lullymore Bog I was sent to Ballygar on the Galway/ Roscommon borders. At that time Bord na Mona were taking over bogs throughout the country and I was designated six bogs, that were owned by Galway County Council situated between Mountbellew and Ballinasloe. I was issued with a 500cc motor cycle as a means of transport. The winter of 1947 was the worst winter in living memory, with snow still on some of the mountains in May, so you can imagine some of the difficulties getting around. Michael Dillon was ganger and he had responsibility for some of the bogs. As well being a ganger, Dillon was also the director of elections for Mark Killilea, a Fianna Fail politician. My boss, Sam Holt, was based in Galway city. Ballygar was a sleepy town, and I stayed in the same hotel as Joe Sweeney who was a school teacher. One aspect of my job was identifying the boundaries, as, unlike Lullymore, some bogs had many owners, and Bord na Mona only owned certain sections. This is when I discovered a new word for my vocabulary – 'mearn.' I would often be told, 'you can't cross that mearn,' as it was a privately-owned part of the bog.

While I was in Ballygar I was sent, with some other supervisors, to test a new semi-automatic turf cutting machine in a bog near Spiddal. While we were in Spiddal we practised our Irish and stayed in digs together. The digs were very rigid, with an 11 p.m. curfew. One night I went to a ceili while the others were in the pub of Mairtin Thornton's, the boxer's. As I wasn't drinking I was the only one back before the curfew, and went to bed. Later that night I heard stones being thrown up at my bedroom window. It was the lads, so I stupidly got up, went down and let them in. As we headed upstairs the lady of the house caught us and said we had to leave. To avoid being thrown out we had to work on her daughter the next day. We spoke to her first thing

51

in the morning and somehow she convinced her mother to allow us to stay.

We had been working on the new Danish made 'De Smitchke' machine for a couple of days, when one afternoon who did we see walking across the bog, only Frank Aiken, a former minister in the recently defeated government. We knew him from his photographs and when he came over I said 'hello Mr. Aiken'. He enquired about the new machine and its suitability for this type of bog. I outlined the process for him having spent a lot of time familiarising myself with the advanced production techniques being used by Bord Na Mona. It was explained to Mr. Aiken that this particular machine wasn't as labour saving as some of the other devices in use at the time as it had to be manually fed. Trying for himself Frank picked up a shovel and fed the machine some turf, 'I see what you mean' he replied. We found out later the reason he had been out there, even though Fianna Fail had been defeated, he still had an interest in the development of the bogs as a natural resource.

I became friendly with a man named Sean Naughton, who was from Mount Talbot which was across the border in Roscommon. I played a bit of hurling for the local team but Sean convinced me to go and play for his crowd, 'Four Roads' in Roscommon. Because of this, every Sunday I would see his father after 12 o'clock Mass and he'd invite me over for dinner insisting 'You must, Sean says you're to come down', so every Sunday afterwards was spent going down to Naughtons for my dinner.

In 1947 Kilkenny were in the All-Ireland hurling semi-final against Galway and I attended with a crowd of Galway people whom I had gotten to know through work. With half an hour to play Galway had them beaten all ends up and it looked like Kilkenny would lose, but in the second half Galway started fouling and Jimmy Langton and Terry Leahy pointed every free they got. Kilkenny came back and eventually won, which meant they were in the all-Ireland final against Cork in Dublin.

On the day of the All-Ireland final I travelled from Galway to Dublin and met with up a crowd from Graignamanagh. It was a big day for us as, 'the Diamond' Hayden from Skeaghvasteen, from my own parish of Graignamanagh, was playing full-back

5 | THE CIVIL SERVICE

Having successfully secured the position of assistant preventive officer in Customs and excise, myself and some other new entrants from the exam reported to the Collector in the Customs House, Dublin. When the Collector had received the particulars required we were taken to a store and issued with our uniforms which consisted of a cap and a long, black waterproof coat. I questioned how this could be regarded as a uniform, having spent six years in the army I knew what a proper uniform was. Some of the other entrants also made some negative comments about the garments.

We were then dispatched to the various stations in Dublin port to begin our 'on the job' experience. This entailed slotting in with a range of duties as we worked under the supervision of a preventive officer. We spent most of our time at No 2 Station which was a very busy place. The B&I boats coming in from Liverpool and the Isle of Man berthed at this area. Clearing passengers' baggage was one of our principal duties. The heavy baggage was handled down at a lower level. I was on duty at the lower level one day when a senior A.P.O. ordered me to 'chalk' some of the cases. I understood that it was necessary to have the owner present before this could be done so I refused. He seemed to be annoyed.

A few days later I was on the higher level dealing with passengers' hand luggage when the C.P.O. approached me during a visit and pointed out that I was not in my proper uniform as I was not wearing my coat at the time. I replied that I hadn't been issued with a 'proper' uniform and pointed out the cycle park attendants who could be seen working outside wearing similar outfits to the preventive staff. This comment wasn't well received and I was a marked man from that day on.

During the work experience we also visited Dublin Airport and Dundalk to observe the mobile patrols and the railway station. The basic-wage for A.P.O. at the time was around £6 per week. I took digs in Glasnevin but soon moved into An Stad in North Frederick street, around the corner from the National Ballroom.

Pearse McMahon, Tom McInerney and myself would go there at the weekends.

Early in '49 during our training, the new Preventive Staff Training Centre opened in Dublin Castle. Myself, J.P McMahon, J.S. Egan, J.C. Daly, C. Desmond, M. Sheridan, M.B. Trimble, J.A. Whelan and T. McInerney were the first students to be taught there. O'Doherty, the superintendant over the preventive staff, had taken a dislike to me because of my previous comment about the lack of a proper uniform. He supervised the training centre. While we were there, however, we were issued with a proper uniform minus a shirt which we were required to provide for ourselves and which we were encouraged to wear with a black tie. Our instructors were Tom McCarthy and Norman Halliday, both P.O.'s. Two good guys the first thing they did was to encourage us to join the Preventive Staff Association as we could not have a trade union. Through Mc Carthy and Haliday I became more interested in the association and learned to appreciate its value.

Mr. R. N. Halliday, Instructor at the Training Centre, explaining flag signals to two trainees, Messrs. O Shea and Whelan. Courtesy 'Irish Times'

I also learned to accept the reality that we, the preventive staff, were the Cinderellas of the service. The landing staff seemed to occupy a more privileged position and enjoyed better working conditions. But the real stumbling block to equality was the standard of education required for the entrance exam for preventive staff. Ours was 7th grade while the landing staff requirement was Leaving Cert. Although all of us had our

Leaving Cert the entry level requirement meant that we could be paid lower wages than the landing staff.

There were other disadvantages too, like not being eligible for children's allowances (Circular E355 dated 16/03/1932, a childrens allowance increase to £15 for all grades did not apply to the preventive staff), or the same amount of holidays, plus the constant jibes about our inferior status. From day one the association began to look for the entrance exam standard to be raised to reflect the important and varied range of duties performed by our members. It happened eventually.

From Dublin to Omeath

There was an exam at the end of the course which I completed in good time, so with 20 minutes remaining I decided to leave early. The results of the exam came out and I was informed by Doherty that I had done 'alright'. At this stage I received my commission as an officer of Customs and Excise which was signed by the Revenue Commissioner authorising me to carry out all allocated duties. On the 27th of April 1949, I was informed in writing that the Revenue Commissioners had ordered my appointment, at State expense, to Omeath, which was on the east coast near Carlingford in Co. Louth. A colleague, Mick Trimble, was also bound for the border. We packed our books of instruction, got our gear together and headed for Connolly Railway Station.

We boarded the Enterprise train en route to Dundalk which was a special train service linking the two cities Dublin and Belfast. The hour's journey gave us the chance to exchange views on what lay ahead. Mick told me that O'Doherty gave him the result of our final test. We were top of the class but I was not to be informed. Our knowledge of the border was very limited so we looked forward to the job as a challenging adventure. As Mick was bound for Clones we said our goodbyes when we reached Dundalk and he switched to the Irish North Rail. I had to change over to the Dundalk/Greenore/Newry line which travelled over the old metal bridge along the northern coast of Dundalk Bay and on through the Cooley peninsula to Omeath. There was a stop at Greenore to allow the engines to turn around. Passengers used this opportunity to have afternoon tea at the hotel which adjoined the platform. When the train was ready to recommence its journey, Tommy Carroll the guard, came out and ushered us all back on the train and we set off for Carlingford and Omeath, the land of legend.

The scenery approaching Carlingford was beautiful with spectacular panoramic views. Maeves Gap of Táin Bó Cúailnge fame was the first to come into view on the summit of Barnavave, it was here the legendary queen of Connacht encamped while her army prepared for its fate. Next we were in the shadow of the majestic Slieve Foye. Stopping briefly in Carlingford to let off a few passengers, we then moved on to Omeath. Leaving Carlingford we passed by the ruins of the 12th century 'Caisleán Rí Sheáin' (King Johns Castle) standing on a rocky outcrop dominating the vast expanse of the lough. Travelling further along the southern shore, we could see the mighty mountains of Mourne across the lough. An Cloch Mor, perched high on the slopes of Slieve Meel, could be seen. Legend tells the giant stone was tossed across Carlingford Lough from the mountains opposite during a fight between the mythical Fionn mac Cumhaill and his archrival Ruscaire, the Ice Giant.

Carlingford Station.

As we approached Omeath you could see ferry boats coming and going from Warrenpoint, and you could see huts which were lined up along the pier selling their goods. When we finally stopped at the station and disembarked I noticed two men waiting on the platform, one older man in plain clothes and a younger man in full uniform. I went over and introduced myself to the older man, Pat Carroll, my new boss, who looked me up and down and said 'You'll do!' I wasn't impressed, here I was, a fine cut of a lad after doing six years in the army and this guy was telling me 'I'll do'. But that was his form, he was that kind of character. The younger man beside him in uniform was Donal O' Brien, an assistant preventive officer. As we made our way to the general office up at the cross in Omeath, side-cars passed us by taking visitors on trips along the coast and there was a holiday atmosphere about the place.

When we got there we chatted for awhile and I found out that there were five A.P.Os in Omeath, Dick Jacob, Tom Ryan, Martin Batell 'Mac Concatha', Donal O'Brien and myself. Donal O'Brien informed me he had my digs fixed up and explained where they were. Pat told me what time I was on at in the morning. Leaving for my digs, we went out the road on bicycles, Donal and myself, cycling through a field and across a railway line, down onto the shore and eventually arriving at a small cottage. Mrs MacDonald, the landlady, was there to greet us. She was a lovely woman, and I settled in from day one. Being so close to the shore the tide would nearly come in the front door at times and I remember having a swim one day when Donal shouted out to me 'Hey, what time is it?' Looking down at my wrist for the answer I was wearing my watch out in the tide!

Mrs MacDonald had a cat that would walk into the dining room everyday and disappear up the chimney only to stroll back in again some minutes later. This particular day the cat came in, doing his rounds, and true to form disappeared up the chimney. Donal hated cats and being ready this day he placed a bundle of paper into the fireplace and put a match to it. I don't know whether the cat ever came back or not. We didn't consider this digs to be suitable for the approaching winter and were looking for something in Omeath. Mrs McDonald then told us she would be leaving which made it easier to change. Mrs Nellie O'Dowd, who was originally from Liverpool, took us in at no 3 Alma Terrace in Omeath. Her husband Alfie was one of the transferred Waterguard in 1923. He died in the early 1930s.

Nellie was a good cook and a lovely lady. She made a home from home for us and fed us very well. She charged very little however, so myself and Donal insisted that she increased her fee. In later life, when I got married, my wife Joan and I visited her regularly and when she could no longer fend for herself we helped her to find an old peoples home. Nellie said she prayed each night for Charlie Haughey and Mr Lynch in thanks for her pension. We continued to visit her until she passed away.

Omeath was a busy station. It was made up of Ferryhill frontier post, the railway frontier post and the ferry service to Warrenpoint. Export controls were still in force. There was full employment in Northern Ireland and the people had money to spend. Certain goods that were in short supply in Northern Ireland were available in the Republic. Omeath like all the border towns played host to a regular influx of day trippers who came by road, rail and ferry.

The ferry service at Narrow Water Castle was run by the Hall family who owned the Ferry Wood and some land on the southern side of the lough. Local people made a living carrying passengers across this narrow bit of water. Passengers paid 2d to cross but with the arrival of motor boats the fare increased to 6d. Small flat bottomed 'punts', which could be operated at low tide, were also used to convey livestock. The fare started at 1d per animal and finished at 10d however I don't remember livestock being ferried during my time. Further down the shore was Grants Harbour, home to the boat families. It was here the Alcorn brothers built their boats including the 15ft punts for which they were famed.

Ferry and Narrow Water Castle.

Many returning day trippers would be laden down with such

goods as butter, sugar, cigarettes, spirits and wearing apparel all of which were liable to seizure. They used every trick in the book at concealment and it was a constant battle of wits between them and us. We came to identify most of the hardcore professionals who were difficult to detect. There were some confrontations worth recording, for example on one occasion I spotted a nervous looking woman on the quay at the Narrow Water ferry crossing. The boatman was waiting for the tide to come alongside. As I drew closer, the woman, who may have had butter or sugar in her bag, seemed to become more agitated. 'Don't come near me or I'll jump in', she shouted. Using a hand gesture, the boatman signalled to me that the woman was unstable so I calmly replied 'Don't do it until the tide comes in'! I let the woman off with a warning instructing her not to do that type of thing again.

After a short while on the job there was a realization that here I was, on the land frontier enforcing customs regulations, and I didn't know too much about the border except what I learned in school and in the training centre. It didn't conform to any natural feature instead it ran along an invisible line through farms, townlands and even houses. The only clear indicator of the border for locals, was where it intersected the roads, as the Northern authorities had better roads as far as the border, while the roads south of the border were never as well maintained. Even the authorities had difficulties at times as was the case with Judge K. Deale who, on the 7th May 1956, was welcomed when he made his first appearance on the bench at Dundalk Circuit Court to adjudicate on three Customs appeal cases. The *Dundalk Democrat* reported that he allowed the appeal and dismissed the prosecution in all three cases. In one case he made a 'landmark' decision when he refused to accept an Ordnance Survey officer's evidence regarding the actual location of the border. Evidence had been given by the prosecution that 20 fat pigs were about to be driven through a fence that was the boundary, into Northern Ireland. For the prosecution, Thomas Gunne, Ordinance Survey Department, stated that he had examined the area in question and its physical features, and when compared with the map they were correct. Judge Deale however, having quoted authorities, said that 'all Mr Gunne had proved was that the physical features of the map where the same now as when the map was made, but how could the man who made the map say where the boundary was' ? This unique judicial perspective of certain fundamental facts was perplexing. Thankfully he stopped short of requesting that we dig up the Boundary Commissioners. It was an unusual ruling at the time. Fuelling my interest in how this border came into existence, I embarked on some research.

6 | THE BORDER

The setting up of the border had been a very difficult and complex undertaking. When the British Government passed the Government of Ireland Act of 1920 it essentially partitioned the country into Northern Ireland and Southern Ireland. The British had no experience of any land frontiers and as the border did not conform to any natural or geographical feature it made the task that bit more difficult. When the Anglo/Irish Treaty was signed in 1921 all public servants in Southern Ireland were directed to remain at their posts. In the interim the British revenue officials were to act as agents for the Southern State and collect all monies due.

Early in 1922, Michael Collins, Minister for Finance attended his second meeting at the colonial office in London. One important matter for discussion eas the revenue collectionn system to be introduched in the new state and the personnel whi were to implement it. Present were a number of senior people from the british revenue office. They agreed tp aprticipate and help the Irish install this system. it was estimated that 400 of all ranks would be required by the new administration. 300 voluntered and the balance were to be trasfereed.

Churchill and Collins seemed to respect each others position. He showed Collins the 1899 Pretoria reward of £25.00 for his head during the Boer war and contrasted it with the £5000.00 on Collins ead twenty five years later.

Collins had plenty of knowledge of the British Services as his sister was married to a revenue offical by the name of Powell who was stationed in Cork.

In 1922, Collins relinguished his post as Minister for Finance and went to Cork to investigate some matters. While in Cork, Collins wrote to Mt. Cosgrave sugesting that three people of statue should be selected to a board to complete the revenue hierachy.

While in Cork he sent an oral message via an intermediary "tell Winston, we could never have done anything without him" Michael Coolins had a nephew "Col. Sean Collins Powell". I served under him when he became Curragh commander in 1944.

On February 21st 1923, Government Order 2/23 became law. It stated there would be a single board of Revenue Commissioners consisting of three commissioners. William O'Brien, a native of Co. Limerick, was appointed first chairman. Charles Joseph Flynn and William Denis Carey were nominated as the two commissioners. Both commissioners were Corkmen. All three had backgrounds in either the UK Inland Revenue or Customs & Excise services. The Revenue Commissioners were born.

Members of the Boundary Commission,
early 1920s, Clady, Urney, Co Tyrone, Richard Feetham S A Jurist.

There were a number of areas known as 'Collections' in existence in the new State responsible for the collection of taxes and duties. There were two collectors that dealt with the border region. The collector in Galway was responsible for two C.P.O. districts, Lifford and Ballyshannon. The Collector in Dublin was responsible for the Dundalk and the Clones districts. Those districts had various stations located throughout, manned by the preventive staff. Under the Revenue Commissioners, staffing structures are listed below in descending order of importance:

Superintendents
Collectors
Surveyors
Officers (Landing staff)

Chief Preventive Officers
Preventive Officers
Assistant Preventive Officers and Auxiliary Preventive men

On the 1st April 1923, although still not fully defined, the land frontier was established and it became necessary to deploy the staff to control the traffic at frontier posts and road stations. It was important that the Government now inform the public of the new restrictive laws that were about to be implemented. Mr. Joe Kieran C.P.O. was in charge in Dundalk. He was to oversee the implementation of the new arrangements which would prove to be a learning process for both the Preventive staff and all cross-border traders. Documentation had to be explained thoroughly and the necessary forms made available. The agreed arrangement was that the carrier would present the merchandise and its covering documentation at the frontier post which would operate between 9 a.m. and 5 p.m.. The goods would be rough checked and compared with the documents and then the transaction was recorded in a book provided. The original documents would be returned to the carrier with duplicates being retained at the frontier post. The carrier would then be instructed to proceed direct to the road station and arrive before 5 p.m. to have the merchandise cleared. These restrictive times however, caused confusion for some members of the public and were gradually extended. Special requests were required to deal with merchandise after 5 p.m.

The staff required to man the Border was assembled in Dublin. It was a motley bunch. The Waterguard would appear to be the obvious choice but volunteers didn't provide the required numbers with some refusing to be assigned to the land frontier. This left the Revenue Commissioners with no option but to take on people without a Customs background. Some members of the preventive staff from the south agreed to work on the border and played a very important role in collecting much needed revenue for the state. This was in spite of the fact that they, the Preventive Staff, had to work under very primitive conditions, in isolated places and without proper accommodation.

There was an attempt at the time to establish a branch of Whitlyism, a workers association similar to that across the water, but Michael Collins is alleged to have said the fledgeling state couldn't afford the luxury of having workers' organisations. From the very beginning, the Revenue Commissioners did not take into consideration the value of the work being done by us when our position was being assessed. The Government had a preference for ex-military people which gave the ex Free State Army and old I.R.A. an opportunity to apply. Sam Sally, Pat Carroll and Frank Hayes were part of the motley group sent to man the border. Sam Sally had received his directions from the Collector General in Dublin via a letter printed on 'Her Majesty's' stationery no less, appointing him to the Border.

Sam Sally's appointment from the Collector.

In Pat Carroll's case he tells the story that he had his passage paid to Canada and by accident he met H. McKinley in Dublin port. McKinley told Pat that he was applying for one of the jobs in the Customs Service and suggested that Pat should do likewise. Pat agreed and joined the crowd waiting to be vetted. He had to listen to the ex-British soldiers relating their experiences on the western front, real 'John Wayne' stuff. Pat was satisfied to keep his own experiences in the Fourth Northern Division of the I.R.A. to himself. They were seeking volunteers for the Border. The 'John Waynes' were silent. Both Pat and Frank Hayes agreed to take on the job and were dispatched to Dundalk to report to Joe Kieran. Joe Kieran had a motorbike as a means of travel and when he discovered that Frank Hayes was a bit of a mechanic he retained his services at Dundalk.

Pat was instructed to take up duty at Annaghvacky Patrol Station which covered the unapproved road to Crossmaglen. Pat, adorned with armband, set out for his station only to discover on arrival that it had been blown up the previous night. The arrangements for the land frontier obviously did not meet with universal approval. Pat returned to Dundalk to await some kind of replacement shelter to be provided at Annaghvacky and used this time to familiarize himself with the customs documentation that would be in use on the border. A tiny paragraph, in 'Revenue Over the Years', asked a very pertinent question: "Against this backdrop, the reader might well ask why anyone would consider working for the Revenue Commissioners. But there were other considerations and compensations".

The official side might list 'seizure rewards' as one of these compensations, the origins of which is shrouded in mystery. It may have been something the English used for officers in small ports, for example they may have gotten an amount per bottle of spirits seized. Our administration introduced similar rewards here. It was very haphazard in its application however, and did not invoke any extra devotion to duty. The record in the appendix outlines a reward of £3.06 included in my salary on 29/03/1979, referring to a seizure made 5 years earlier on 28/02/1974. It was hardly worth the wait. I don't remember what I received for the record seizure of cigarettes in 1969. I would accept however, that despite some primitive conditions and shabby treatment, the Preventive staff were not deskbound and did have a great variety of exciting duties as compensations also, and this was also the view held by retired members.

One of the first incidents Pat Carroll had to deal with in Annaghvacky was a man he found taking coal on a horse and cart across the border. When Pat challenged him the man said, 'I've been conveying coal from Dundalk to Crossmaglen since I was fifteen.' Pat told him that he may not be aware, but there had some changes since then and would be obliged if the man would complete the appropriate Customs forms but the man refused. Pat recognized from the nameplate on the man's cart that he was a native of South Armagh. As Pat was also from South Armagh he used this coincidence to strike up a conversation. Although the man still refused to sign he did concede to putting an X on the form.

An officer named Paddy Bennett was credited with making the first seizure on the border in 1923 and was still serving in 1949 when I took up my own appointment. At the time the district justice, Mr Mac Eachach, in his summing up stated that we had been paying our taxes to a foreign government but we were now legally and morally bound to pay the new taxes. In future there would be no excuses for any offence and he would impose the maximum fine.

Donal O'Brien (retired Customs Officer) & Jim O'Shea 2010.

Ferryhill Customs Post 1949. (We both served there in 1949).

8 | OMEATH

In the Dundalk area there were three approved road border crossings with frontier posts in position. Carrickcarnan frontier post was on the main Belfast-Dublin Road. Drumbilla frontier post was on the Armagh Dundalk road and controlled the merchandise traffic for Dundalk road station. Ferryhill frontier post was on the Newry-Omeath road and served Greenore road station. Staff worked an 8 hour day, 48 hour week. Working hours were dictated by the needs of the frontier post with staff working various shifts known as 'schemes of attendance'. Each officer got this scheme a week in advance.

It was important that we control the Border efficiently, we were, after all, a new state, the survival of which was dependent on the collection of taxes and duties. Across the Border, was the British Commonwealth, and no matter how much was smuggled into its six counties, it would make no impact on the economy of Britain. Smuggling in the other direction however, from Britain into Ireland, even on a small scale, defrauded the state of vital revenue which in turn could have had a disastrous effect on the country's finances.

During my first week Pat had me working beside the regular staff enforcing customs regulations and helping me fit in as one of the five A.P.Os running the station. During this time I got my separate run of duty which happened to be at Ferryhill frontier post. For the purposes of monitoring the border, both administrations had agreed to recognise a number of cross Border roads as 'approved' for carrying merchandise. Motor vehicles, which were also classed as merchandise, were confined to these approved roads. All other roads were deemed 'unapproved' and merchandise was prohibited. The only concession was exempt farm produce which was not liable for duty or restriction, conveyed by horse and cart. Doctors and the clergy were also exempt and got a special pass.

Carrickcarnan frontier post closed at midnight with smaller frontier posts like Ferryhill and Drumbilla closing at 9 p.m.. Opening at 8 a.m., goods and vehicles passing through the approved route at Ferryhill frontier post had to be documented and controlled. The scheme of attendance or work shifts were 8 a.m. to 4 p.m. and 1 p.m. to 9 p.m.. All motor vehicles crossing the Border required a pass. On the northern side they didn't stamp vehicles, however on our side a record of all entries and exits were recorded in a book. Drivers travelling in either direction would come to the office to get their pass-book checked, stamped and initialled. Afterwards I would examine their vehicle and let them away. People declaring merchandise would come 'under control' at the frontier post, where a record of the goods being carried was recorded and kept. They were then directed to the road station in Greenore where the goods were further examined and the appropriate tariff calculated, on receipt of which they were cleared. One frequent cross-border traveller was Eddie Filgate. He served in Bord na Mona and we would often compare notes when we met in Dundalk. He created history by being one of three Fianna Fáil TDs elected for Louth in 1977.

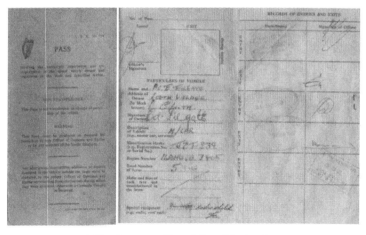

A Border pass, Republic of Ireland.

Temporary Border pass, Northern Ireland.

While on duty, I was asked by Pat about my time in the Fifth Motor Squadron. He asked me whether I would be able to handle the patrol car and I replied 'I suppose we could take a chance'. So here he had me as a driver even though I wasn't officially passed to drive, it became just part of the job. My workmates were all good company; as well as Donal O'Brien there was Dick Jacob, Tom Ryan, and Martin Battell, who, like me, had been in the army. We liked to socialise and Doyle's pub was a great meeting spot, particularly on pay days, as there was no bank to cash your cheque. It was, however, an expensive way to cash a cheque as it would cost you a round, and there could be six or seven lads there at any one time. I wasn't a drinker, and couldn't drink more than a bottle of lemonade, but Donal O' Brien, who didn't drink either, would go round for round with the lads, just drinking lemonade. Tom Ryan used to say jokingly that he didn't mind buying a lad a drink but he couldn't bring himself to buy lemonade - it was only fit for children!

Weekly patrol sheets were made out in advance and identified the times and places to be visited. Both the C.P.O. and staff got copies of this list each Monday. The P.O. would accompany each patrol. The limit of the Omeath patrol was Gyles Quay including all the intervening inlets including Ballagan, Templetown and Whitestown. Grant's Harbour and Greer's Quay were also visited. The Flagstaff and Longwomans Grave got special attention.

The land frontier regulations gave the Customs patrols authority to stop and search all vehicles within twenty miles of the border. Outside of this twenty mile zone it would require special circumstances to engage in a search i.e. a follow up chase. I had only been in Omeath a few days when Pat came into the office and asked me to drive him to Greenore that night to collect a hundred pound fine that had been imposed on a man for a Customs offence. He told me that the man was 'a big fisherman from across in Greencastle in Northern Ireland' and referred to him as 'a rough diamond' who could be dangerous. 'Whats more' he said 'this fella has only one good eye, the other one is glass', Handing me a baton he said 'if you see a sparkle in the good eye, you close it with a belt of that baton'! A nice introduction to the job I thought. We headed over to Greenore, parking in the grounds of the hotel and headed for the bar. We were nearly there when Pat told me he had left the receipt book in the car. When I returned with the receipt book, the two of them, Pat and Matt McVeigh, were having a drink like they were long lost cousins. Pat had the hundred pound in his hand and asked me to make out the receipt. On the way back I asked Pat if he was having me on about Mc Veigh being dangerous. He assured me he was not. 'You always have to be on your guard with smugglers', he advised. I later saw in the records that McVeigh had once assaulted a Customs official, Jim Ryan, in Carlingford.

Another day the Higher Collector, Mr Neligan, arrived down to Ferryhill on inspection, accompanied by Pat. He asked me how I liked the job and replying I said it had great variety but I felt that we should be paid more for the work we were doing. He questioned me about what I worked at before. I told him I had been an officer in the army and had worked in Bord na Mona. 'Bord na Mona' ? he replied, 'You must have been one of the Fianna Fail pets to get a job there'. I said 'Excuse me! I joined the army in 1940 for 13s and 2 pence a week and served for six years. My record entitled me to participate in any of the jobs that were available'. He turned to Pat Carroll and said 'I don't want to get any further into this discussion', and then left. Pat Carroll, who was there during the conversation, later said that I had stood up to him well.

The smuggling in Omeath was mainly confined to petty smuggling of foodstuffs, whiskey and cigarettes. While the main traffic was from the south to the north, tea, which was scarce here after the war, was smuggled from the north to the south. Superior quality razor blades were also brought south as we had an inferior class razor blades called a Max Smile. Onions were also a frequently smuggled commodity as well as 'sprig nails' which were used in the boot trade. The markets decided from year to year which items were most lucrative to smuggle and in which direction they would travel. For example in 1940, sprig nails cost 10 shillings per stone in Northern Ireland whereas in the south the cost was much higher at £3 per stone, onions cost £14 per ton in Kerry whereas in London the price was £90 per ton. Illegal onion exports created a huge amount of copy for the *Dundalk Democrat*, much of it humorous such as the following: 'One lad is reputed to have cleaned up £400 in a week. He made £180 in one day with a few fast runs and when he had paid for drinks all round he took off his hat to the hitherto despised onion and listed it first in the list of good things that came from the earth. Once he said, the sight of an onion brought tears to his eyes but now the tears were those of gratitude and thankfulness'. Onion smuggling came to a sudden end however, in early November 1940. As the report went: 'One morning out of a particularly blue sky there came a totally unexpected bolt. Some all-powerful big-wig over in London sent out a four line paragraph that in his opinion 4½d per pound was a fair price at which to sell onions in England and Northern Ireland. This notice knocked the bottom out of the onion market. There was no more money in the business thereafter'.

When we made a seizure, the procedure was to record it in the seizure register. A report was then sent to 'Division Two' of the Revenue Commissioners office in Dublin Castle. When writing the report you had to bear in mind that if the case went to court the decision to prosecute would be based, in the main, on the contents of your report. Having received the report the Revenue Commissioners would assign a C&E file number to the case, and come back to us with the decision. The official decision was then recorded in the seizure register, along with a record of disposal of seized goods.

While many goods were smuggled in the panels of car doors, under seats, or in the spare-wheel well, one of the most common means of smuggling was by train in womens' underskirts. We had no lady searchers in Omeath and women took full advantage. Cigarettes and butter were the main items smuggled. Some women had special underskirts made, fitted with pockets for the purpose of smuggling. You could see the goods swaying in their skirts as they walked along the platform, but you couldn't do anything about it. The drill for female foot-passengers was to first ask if they had any goods concealed on their person. You then sent them into the office, requesting that they remove any items they may be concealing. G.N.R. provided the office on the platform and buckets of coal from the train kept us topped up which meant we always had a good fire.

One cold and wet winter's day, a group of women were waiting to board the train. The train was late and the women were huddled together shivering from the cold. I went through the usual procedure and when I send them into the office they were more than happy to oblige, as it allowed them shelter from the elements. Now, there was a great big stove in the office and on this particular day I had the fire blazing. Butter and cigarettes were the most smuggled items at that time and I suspected that the heat of the stove would melt whatever butter the women were concealing. The women said nothing until they got on the train, then some of them put their heads out the window and shouted, 'Ye De Valera's bastard'! Was this a new form of Revenue Protection? On reflection I didn't think so. It was a once-off in Omeath even though this method may have been used elsewhere.

Canon O'Hehir was one of our regular 'customers' at the Ferryhill frontier post. On one occasion he was found to have whiskey hidden in the car. Bill Butler, the officer on duty, rather than seizing the goods, gave the Canon the opportunity of taking the whiskey back to the pub so that he could get his money back.

The Canon agreed and when he returned Bill waved him through. However, when he reached the far side he was stopped by the British customs and the whiskey, which he was still carrying, was seized. At the time Bill Butler was due for promotion, but when the headquarters heard about the incident, his promotion was deferred.

The Canon was persona non grata after, but the incident did not deter him from trying to pull another stunt soon after. This time, he arrived with his house keeper sitting in the rear seat of the car. Donal O'Brien, who was the officer on duty, asked him if he had any goods to declare, to which he replied that he had not. Donal then directed the same question to the lady in the back. Before she had a chance to answer, the Canon snapped, 'Didn't I tell you I don't have any goods to declare' ? Donal ignored the Canon's remark and asked the lady to step out of the car. The minute she did it was obvious that she was concealing a number of bottles of whiskey. Donal told the Canon that he was seizing the whiskey. 'I'll put horns on if you do' ! said the Canon. 'If you put horns on me, Canon, ' said Donal, 'you'll be the first person I'll puck with them" !

Even though we, as revenue officers, had a job to do, we always tried to be mindful of the fact that the Border was a terrible imposition on the people of Omeath with Newry being their natural place for socialising and shopping. This realisation demanded that you be as diplomatic as possible, while still letting them know who was boss from time to time. However, it was inevitable that you would sometimes incur the displeasure of certain members of the community.

The social life in Omeath was nondescript but the place would come to life once every year when the bachelors dance I took place. Requests or 'demands' as some officers referred to them, were introduced to facilitate the social life for border residents. The motorist would be required to make this request during working hours, fill out the prerequisite form and pay the fee of 2 shillings. Often the request was for 3 a.m. or some other anti-social hour. In this instance the officer's attendance to facilitate the crossing would be 3-4 a.m. as the traveller was given one hours grace. For his trouble the officer was given 2 hours overtime pay for this 3-4 a.m. attendance. This extra money

75

was appreciated but hard-earned. Imagine a lone officer sitting in a tin shack of a frontier post at that late hour, out in the middle of nowhere. After finishing the A.P.O. would then take his road signs in, douse the fire, if he had one, and cycle home, which was often several miles away.

While signing on one morning at 8 a.m. at the office in Omeath, I was visited by Mr O Doherty, a Preventive Superintendent from Dublin. He informed me that he was down to investigate a complaint made against Mr. Martin MacConcatha. He was sarcastic about Martin's use of the Irish version of his name and asked why I wasn't using mine. I told him mine was too long. He had stayed overnight in a local hotel and was carrying out an early morning inspection. His sarcastic attitude didn't augur well for Martin who was issued with a warning for being discourteous to a member of the public, a 'request' was the issue.

On another occasion I seized goods from one particular family who lived in Omeath and had a business across the Border in Newry. We had information that the family car had a major overhaul including a new set of Michelin x tyres, which were much sought after at the time. On a Monday it was decided to give them a chance to pay the duty owed on the repairs by asking the driver the usual questions on each entry. If they didn't declare the repairs by the end of the week, the officer on duty that Friday was to apply the regulations. I was on duty that Friday when the son came in during my spell. When questioned he denied having any repairs done to the car. Having first examined both the car and its tyres, I explained that it was liable to seizure but that he would be given the opportunity to pay T.D.V. (treble the duty paid value). When I calculated the fine I was challenged by the son, who questioned how I arrived at the figure commenting that I didn't look as if I had sufficient intelligence to do it. I told him that he was the last man to talk about intelligent looks and that we should carry on with the business at hand. At that point he called on his father who was out in the car. The father came in and I found myself on the receiving end of some flowery language, 'is this what we fought for' etc. Eventually he produced his cheque book. I apologised saying that we could not accept cheques in these circumstances. His language was no longer flowery and he erupted. He stated that he had 'friends in high places' and he would have me transferred by phone. I outlined the facts in my report and didn't hear anything from on high afterwards.

The next time I stopped them at the frontier post I found them reciting the rosary, so I joined in on the Holy Mary. 'Now' I said, 'we've done our bit for the man above, now let's deal with the state, ! One of our jobs was to examine the parcel post. I was working in the post office one day when a son of theirs, a newly-ordained priest, arrived in. He said that he believed that his family had a disagreement with me, but he also understood that the job I was doing had to be done. He then gave me his blessing. That was the way it was in Omeath - both the officers and the community had to find a way of co-existing, and by and large we did.

While you were normally dealing with locals and visitors from over the Border, occasionally preventive officers came across people travelling from abroad. I was on duty one evening at Ferryhill frontier post when who arrived only Brendan Behan! We knew each other from the previous encounters. 'Holy Jesus, Jim,' he said to me, 'is it yourself' ? 'It is,' I replied. I asked him where he was coming from and he replied that he was coming from some Socialist International rally in France and had hitched a lift on a boat to Liverpool. He had then taken Fisher's coal boat across to Newry and gotten off at the Victoria Lock gates on the canal. 'Any chance of openers' ? he asked me. What he meant was that he just needed the price of the first drink. I gave him a few shillings and watched him head straight across the road to Buckley's pub. I believe he entertained them all night long. Another famous character I came across at the time was Rinty Monaghan, the world flyweight boxing champion from Belfast. He would stay in the gatehouse to the Park Hotel and it was said that he trained on goat's milk. He had won the championship at this stage but he would still come up and down to Omeath regularly and during a conversation with him one day he was gracious enough to give me his autograph.

Rinty Monaghan.
World Flyweight Champion, Britain, British Empire and European
Champion.

One day after returning by bus from a weekend away in Dublin, I was met at the crossroads by Mrs Carroll, Pat's wife. She asked me had I heard about poor Pat. 'No',I said 'why'? 'They kidnapped him! ' she replied. Apparently he had been on car patrol at Greenore with Jim Ryan and Cathal O'Sandair (of Reics Carlo fame, a character created by Cathal, a well-known writer in Irish) when they came upon some smugglers loading sugar onto a boat. Pat drove on to the beach, in front of Hanley's shop, to apprehend the smugglers. When they saw the lights of the car however two ran away with O'Sandair and Ryan giving chase. The third lad stayed in the boat, which was pulled up on the gravel. Pat had climbed into the boat and began to unload the sugar when, in an effort to escape, the smuggler pushed the boat out to sea. The boat travelled down the coast a little until Pat was forced to step out into the water to avoid kidnap. He had to wade through two feet of water to get ashore and got soaking wet in the process. As we said afterwards 'Luckily it was only his dignity that was injured'. Sometime later we found out who the culprits were and that they were still smuggling so we decided to do a job on them. One night while on patrol, myself and Dick Jacob were let off at Greenore by Pat. We had heard that the smugglers, who were from Greencastle, were bringing in a small boat that night. With no radio communication at that time, Jacob and myself concealed ourselves under some railway wagons at the station. After some time we heard two voices approaching. Both men were carrying sacks. I wanted to challenge them but Dick restrained me saying that they would 'do a second run'. He was right as they left the sacks on the quayside and went away for more. We were ready to tackle them when they returned, some minutes later, with more goods. We had one lad under control, however the second fellow made a break for the boat. Giving chase, I slipped on the greasy wooden steps that lead to the boat, and fell on my man, knocking the wind out of him. 'I'll go sir, I'll go sir' ! he pleaded. Little did he know that I was also winded. We held the smugglers and their sacks, which were full of cigarettes, and signalled to Pat using our torches. This turned out to be the biggest cigarette seizure I would make while in Omeath. The men were subsequently arrested, charged and fined. We were the good boys with Pat afterwards.

Pat Carroll was an unusual fellow and regulations didn't mean much to him. We got a cycle allowance for using our bikes to go to the frontier posts, but one day I found all the claims he should have sent in the glove compartment of the car. Another day the C.P.O. rang to say that three inspectors were en route to Omeath to inspect the station. Pat was at home at the time so I went down to his house and knocked at the door. Pat arrived out in his shirt sleeves, puffing a cigarette from the corner of his mouth. 'The Chief was on', I said, 'There are three inspectors on their way down to inspect the station'. 'Over my dead body, Pat replied, 'take that car out, we're going on patrol'. I took the car out and recorded the departure time and speedometer reading. We travelled to the Ferryhill frontier post where Pat went in and signed the book. We then travelled out to Flagstaff. Half-way out the road Pat told me he'd forgotten to pick up Jim Ryan and that we had to go back to Carlingford for him. When we arrived at Carlingford however the three inspectors were waiting for us. I stayed in the car to finish filling in the log book and journal. After awhile I was called in and asked for my commission, my journal and the log book for the car. When we returned to Omeath the inspectors didn't appear to be too pleased with Pat's record-keeping. I later found out that Jim Ryan had signed on and off at the same time – a very serious offence. My documents in order, which was mentioned, apparently, to the chief in Dundalk and may have influenced a phone call I received from the chief's clerk, Johnny Moon, asking me if I would like to move to Dundalk. I said I would but thought that applying for a transfer would be seen to be disloyal to my colleagues in Omeath. He told me it wouldn't be necessary to make any application, as the chief had the powers to transfer a single person within his own district. This conversation was the beginning of a process which soon saw me move to Dundalk as a member of the mobile patrol staff.

called Dermot O'Reilly. What made the investigation sensitive was the fact that O'Reilly was the brother of P.J. O'Reilly, the surveyor in charge of the Investigation Branch. Dermot O'Reilly refused to answer questions until he contacted his brother in Dublin. The investigation branch then asked that the seizure report be sent directly to their office, but Joe Magee, the CPO in charge of Dundalk district sent the file directly to division two of the Revenue Commissioners office. This displeased P.J. O'Reilly. At the subsequent court hearing, officers from the Dublin investigation branch gave evidence suggesting that Dermot O'Reilly was acting as agent provocateur. The case against him was dismissed and Sheridan was also let go. Kirk was convicted of smuggling and fined £1,628. P.J. O'Reilly became Inspector General afterwards (1958) and I was to have many encounters with him on Association matters.

An early mobile patrol L to r: Johnny McMahon, Jim ("Spud") Murphy, Joe McGee and Pat Langan.

Joe McGee.

In the early to mid-1950s, while still an A.P.O and single, I discovered John Lynch and Spud Murphy were great hands at rearing and training greyhounds. Spud used to run his dogs in Navan and Dundalk and would take a good few scoops from time to time. If he was drinking he would have a bundle of fellas with him but if he wasn't he'd ask me to accompany him. 'Are you doing anything this evening' ? he'd ask. 'No, why' ? I'd reply. 'I want you to drive me to Navan' he'd say. Spud would hire a car from Andy Hanratty on Castletown Road and I'd pick him and the dog up and head for Navan. Before reaching Navan however, Spud would ask me to stop at some lane or gateway. He'd then take the dog out and administer a 'special supplement' before continuing on. We had some good winners. He had a special dog called 'Pointers Prince' which was entered for some important trophy. The Prince won three races to reach the finals. He paid well. The final was to take place in the autumn which meant it would be run under lights. Spud was on the beer so my services were not required. John Lynch, Frank McMenamin and myself travelled to see the race. There was a big crowd at the park. A doggy man from Newry approached us asking about Pointers Prince. I told him that Spud fancied the Prince to win but he replied that his entry would win instead and asked us to advise Spud not to put the 'tank' on as he'd lose. Unfortunately, this advice was lost on Spud. We, however, accepted the tip and backed the Newry dog which won. 'Spud you're that crooked you couldn't lie straight in bed' was the reply Spud received on another occasion from a woman whom Spud had told not to back his dog as it had a bad leg. The dog had won however.

On yet another occasion Spud had one of his greyhounds out for a run on a stretch of land near his home in Pearse Park. The greyhound had run through a fence and badly injured his side on barbed wire in the process. Left in a bad way the dog had to be taken to a vet. John Lynch advised Spud to ignore the local vet's advice to have him put down saying 'he'll be alright, we'll doctor him'. The dog recovered and was in good form when Spud asked me would I take a day off to bring him up to Dublin. He explained that he wanted to take the dog up to Shelbourne Park for trials. I agreed and it was the usual drill, the dog was brought up, won his trials and afterwards he was sold for a good price.

Frank McMenamin, or Franco as he was known, was a likeable character always ready to introduce a controversial topic for debate. He was a native of Co Tyrone and took great delight at tormenting Dennis Farren who was a Donegal man. He would remark to Dennis, they all could be seen coming across the bridge at Lifford with the wee bag over their shoulders. He lived in Pearse Park and was also a sometime doggy man. Franco's wife Briege was a very friendly person and kept an open house for his friends. Franco was unfortunate enough to get gallstones and even though he was in constant pain, was reluctant to have an operation opting instead to try a homeopathic treatment which was prescribed by a lady who claimed to have 'the cure'. This did not work so Briege and I convinced him to go to the old Dundalk hospital at the Crescent. Dr Clarke performed the operation and Franco survived. When he came home he took with him a jar containing the offending gallstones. He placed the stones in the cure he had tried and left them sitting on the kitchen window. Here the jar sat on display for some time much to his wife's annoyance. As the stones had not shrunk I suggested that she should dump them. Sometime later, a crowd of us were in the house when someone brought up Franco's time in hospital. I drew attention to the fact that both the jar and the stones had seemingly melted away in the 'cure'. We had a great laugh about it but Briege told me that I would be barred from the house from then on.

Another important member of the mobile patrols was Frank Hillen, son of Joe Hillen who had been the P.O. in charge of the port and had resided in the Customs House. Frank was a very competent driver and was involved in many seizures one of which created a record as follows. Frank had been on patrol in the Annyalla area of Co Monaghan when a V8 each wagon failed to stop when challenged. The chase began with Frank at the wheel as they travelled all the minor roads in north Monaghan a number of times. The Castleblayney patrol got into the hunt but without radio could not contact the 'hunter'. When they arrived back at Annyalla the beach wagon crossed and re-crossed the border and did a spin through Keady, Newtownhamilton and on up the mountains. One passenger bailed out and the chase re-entered the State. The chase ended when the wagon ran out of petrol. The driver jumped out and ran across country but was captured after some time. Four hours had elapsed since he was called on to stop. The crew described it afterwards as 'just some chase' ! The wagon contained 28 gross drinking glasses (1/2 pint size). Outside of the job Frank and I shared the same doctor who could use strong language on occasion. He was a very good doctor and was set in his ways. The doctor's bill, which could be substantial at times, was received every six months. Frank had called, outside of surgery hours, to settle his bill. Normally the doctor's wife, who was also a doctor, or the maid would answer the door. However on this occasion the doctor himself answered. Frank was met with an impolite greeting to which he equally replied 'Well if that's the f*ing way you feel then you can wait for your money' ! The doctor enjoyed the banter and apologised and all was well.

Frank was an avid golf player and a member of the Dundalk Golf Club. He was buying a new set of clubs so I bought his old set and joined the Club. He went on to teach me course etiquette and enjoying his crack my game improved as time went on.

In one instance there was a cheque addressed to Frank lying at the office for a few days. Liam Ó Gogain decided to take it down to Frank at his home only to find him absent. He gave the cheque to Mrs Hillen letting her know Frank had received money other than salary. Result, big trouble for Frank and even bigger trouble for Liam!

Work continued with most people crossing the Border tempted to smuggle something for their own use. This type of smuggling was never an important target for the mobile patrols which were mainly interested in the professional smuggling fraternity. It was a difficult assignment. Mobile patrols had been a recent innovation introduced by C.P.O. Joe Magee, and gave Preventive Officers more flexibility resulting in a much more effective way of patrolling the Border. This put an end to the 'showing of the flag' effort of 'schemed patrols', which were planned a week in advance and involved being at a certain spot at a certain time.

Patrols rotated between late and early shifts with each crew doing 48 hours per week plus 10 hours overtime, but even at this there was still a big gap left for the smugglers to exploit. Overtime was reluctantly given to us by the Controlling Grade comprising inspectors and collectors, and every overtime claim needed covering sanction before it could be sent for payment. This resulted in needless delays in payment and led to unnecessary conflict between the patrols and the Collector. Aggrieved with this unnecessary imposition, we were convinced that the overtime was not paid in the spirit intended or in good faith. Eventually we curtailed our attendance to 48 hours in protest and when we made a seizure outside the 48 hours and did not claim. The Higher Collector, Waldron, came down to try and settle the affair. There was some straight talking done and a settlement achieved. The overtime claims would be forwarded directly to the Accountant General for payment. The covering sanction was no longer required.

To keep the smugglers guessing we did our best to vary our times and as a result we had some successes and made substantial seizures. Our movements were being monitored however, and our homes and digs were under constant surveillance by the smugglers and their agents in their efforts to identify safe times and gaps for them to smuggle. They soon checked me out as my boss, John G. Walsh, caught a fellow watching me near my digs. He confronted the individual who denied any wrongdoing and we had no powers to take it any further.

This was prior to radio communication and it was interesting to observe the relationship between the patrols and the smugglers. In the early hours one morning we stopped the late P.G. Rice with an empty van and engaged him in conversation. He admitted to being a republican who wanted to see the Border go but, as he succinctly put it, 'not just yet'. Other smugglers looked on us as a 'necessary evil' and rationalised that 'but for us everyone would be at the game and there would be no profit in it'.

The crews of both patrols got a pleasant surprise when we were given two wonderful second-hand cars in excellent condition. The cars had previously been involved in a very large gold seizure. No. 1 patrol got a Dodge and No. 2 patrol received a Chrysler Windsor. The Chrysler was a lovely car to drive and proved lucky over the years when it delivered its share of seizures without any accidents to report. One of the first seizures that took place using the new cars was a large consignment of cigarettes and butter. Coincidentally, the driver of the vehicle containing the illegal consignment was the man whom John G. Walsh had caught watching my digs shortly after I arrived in Dundalk.

On 25th August 1951, we made a significant seizure when 53,000 Player's cigarettes, ½ ton of Sugar and 200 lbs of creamery butter were intercepted. We were expecting the load to come from a premises on Barrack Street, Dundalk, but knew that it would not move until our patrols cars were garaged. The Special Investigation Branch provided two powerful Ford V8 cars for use in the operation on condition that they would not be damaged. Both cars and crew were parked at the vacant Military Barracks with the premises under observation. As instructed I garaged the patrol car before 2 a.m. and went to my digs. At 1.55 a.m. Customs officers observed a motor car emerge without lights, from the premises on Barrack Street. Expecting a clear run it proceeded down Peter Street toward the Point Road and then on to the Blackrock Road. The Customs officers, who were nearly caught out as they had expected the car to go in the opposite direction through the town and out the Newry Road, followed in their patrol cars. The load made its way out through Blackrock, across the Dublin Road at McGeough's Cross and continued across country to Dungooley until it eventually crossed into Northern Ireland by an unapproved road. Despite several attempts it was not possible to get in front of the quarry as it continued its journey over various byroads. They were well into Northern Ireland when they finally forced the car to stop somewhere between Newry and Banbridge. The driver, Daniel Begley from Castletown Road Dundalk, was given the option of coming back to Carrickcarnan or going to the RUC. He agreed to return to Carrickcarnan, perhaps because the penalties imposed in the North were much greater than the South, and was taken back in the patrol car with John Lynch driving the seized load. On the way back, at Cloghoge on the southern side of Newry, a lorry attempted to put the patrol cars off the road, but was unsuccessful. On arrival at Carrickcarnan Pat Langan arrested Begley and he was subsequently taken before Dundalk District Court on 12th September where he was fined £843. Gerry McGeough displayed an interest in the case and it was alleged at the time that he had been the owner of the seized load. This seizure would emerge much later as the foundation for a series of coincidental events but *sin scéal eile*.

Giving evidence in court was an important part of our duties. The first time was a bit of an ordeal however compliance with the judges rules protected you from anything the defence lawyer could throw at you. We were leaving Dundalk Court after giving evidence one day when Francie Meegan, who had just been fined £100 for his involvement in a butter smuggling case, called out to us, 'lads, I'd love to have a drink with you but I have to go and make up that fine with a few pigs!'.

One night, arising from a tip-off, it was decided to do a joint patrol in the Castleblayney area. There had been an earlier seizure involving a pig smuggling operation in this location which was subsequently written up in the local newspaper entitled 'Amphibious Border Pigs. How they negotiate rivers'. We took up positions close to the River Fane and soon heard men approaching. One of our group accidentally flashed his torch prematurely and a scattering match ensued with lads running in all directions, leaving pigs behind them on the road. I grabbed one lad who was running toward a ditch. When he straightened up however he lifted me off my feet. He tried to hit me with an 'ash-plant' but I was too close to him to get hurt. Spud Murphy saw my predicament and intervened with his rubber baton. I felt the smuggler go limp so I relaxed my grip on him. He broke free however kicking me in my stomach as he made good his escape diving through a hedge.

What to do with pigs which had been seized was a big problem. Essentially, it was the responsibility of the Department of Agriculture to dispose of them, but it was always left up to us. This caused problems as on a few occasions, while we were waiting to dispose of the pigs, the smugglers broke into the compound and took their pigs, and lorries, back.

Reflecting on the vast variety of articles and goods that were smuggled over the years, one has to list the humble 'pig' as one of the more constant items that we encountered. There was a time when the poor pig led a domestic, sedentary existence, either as a loner or a member of a herd, with most of its time spent with its snout in a feeding trough. By the 1950s however a big change had taken place in the lifestyle of the humble pig. They became constantly on the move, travelling in groups all over the country. Enjoying frequent trips in big lorries one would think they had no fixed abode as they repeatedly crossed and re-crossed the border without valid passports.

Indeed the poor Customs officer had constant difficulty identifying 'returning residents' from the rest. Consignments of pigs with a special tattoo mark 'M55F' came south and were seized resulting in court proceedings but the movement of pigs continued unabated. The pigs distinguished themselves over time as extremely versatile travellers. They demonstrated the art of crossing streams and rivers with ease and displayed further expertise by skilfully navigating underground tunnels. It was a great show and titles like 'Amphibious Border Pigs' were well earned. The final show was the 'Carousel' sponsored by the Common Agricultural Policy with the same "pigs" being imported and exported on a continous basis.

In April 1953, Johnny Moon, the C.P.O's clerk, died and the chief asked me to take over the vacant position at his office in St. Patricks Hall. My new office duties entailed dealing with and recording all incoming and outgoing correspondence, as well as monitoring the maintenance and life history of each patrol car and its associated fuel bills. With no photocopier or typewriter available all instructions were written in long hand. I was also responsible for recording staffing levels and annual/sick leave.

It had been a quiet afternoon at the office when the sudden arrival of an excited Waterguard officer triggered off some swift action. The officer, who was clearly agitated, asked in a pronounced English accent if I knew an O'Hagan. I Informed him that O'Hagan was an extremely common name in the area. He then went on to explain the reason for his abrupt visit. He had been on patrol at Ballsmill unapproved road when a loaded lorry had come along. Standing in the middle of the road in full uniform he called on the driver to 'Halt in the Queen's name'. He went on to tell me that the 'blighter' had put his head out the window and shouted 'F... u and the Queen' and drove off. They had subsequently given chase but lost the lorry and now required our assistance. I alerted one of our patrols to join the search for the offending 'blighter' who, I was told, was hauling a load of sulphate of ammonia, a prohibited export from N.I. I then explained to the officer that he should not have been so surprised at the response he had gotten as I would probably receive something similar if I called on him to 'halt in Dev's name'.

Taking the job of clerk meant losing overtime, but I was compensated with additional duties at the Dundalk Railway Station. The station had just one main entrance and exit for the public and was made up of two tracks, one northbound and one southbound track. Between these there were a number of offices including the station master's office, the restaurant and bar and a small shop occupied by Easons. After a break in the buildings there was the foreign parcel post and then the Customs and Excise office. The Customs and Excise office had two doors which opened out onto both platforms. Back in the early 1940s the numbers of people coming through Dundalk railway station from the north of Ireland as day trippers grew day by day.

In 1942, during the month of July or thereabouts, the volume of passengers had increased so much that a special team was formed, comprising all available Customs and Excise staff augmented by members of An Garda Siochana, to examine the copious numbers passing through the station to board the Belfast train. Afterwards the *Times* newspaper wrote that over the weekend about 5,000 passengers had been involved and that amongst other items that were taken, between 700-800 pounds of butter were seized. In an effort to control these continuing large numbers a robust structure was created parallel to the north side platform. This corridor channelled the passengers right up to the Customs offices and the examination tables. The sheer numbers and frequency of arrivals also meant that Customs officers rarely had sufficient time to break for tea, which G.N.R. provided for us in the restaurant on the platform. Often leaving an unfinished cup of tea on the restaurant table, we'd rush to board the southbound Enterprise train heading for Dublin and examine the passengers en route. We'd get off at Drogheda station having completed the examination where we would have 30 minutes or so to spare before the northbound Enterprise train en route to Belfast came in from Dublin. On occasion we'd use this interval to engage the station master, Mr Popjoy, in a friendly game of poker. We would then board the northbound train and examine its passengers on the way back to Dundalk. On arrival at Dundalk we'd disembark allowing the passengers waiting to board the train continue their journey. At the railway station I was working with very senior staff who were well able to carry out the duties assigned to them. Some 'wag' referred to the place as 'St Bridget's Ward'. Some of the staff had service in the War of Independence including Paddy Bennett and Frank Hayes whom I mentioned earlier. Benny Walsh was the P.O. and handled this very busy station with liberal efficiency. Included on the staff were Peadar Clancy, a big imposing Corkman, Johnny Gordon and Liam Seery. Records show that both Johnny and Peadar had a number of gold ring seizures.

I noticed that Johnny had some fingers missing. He never mentioned how it happened but seemed to suggest an association with the old I.R.A. in his home in County Leitrim. Spud Murphy said he never heard about him and that perhaps he may have made tea for Cumann na mBan. The truth was that on Christmas Eve, 1942, Johnny had cycled down the ramp at the station full of the seasons good will. When he reached the platform he got a wobble and ended up on the railway track. A passing train ran over his bike and in the process he lost his fingers. He was unable to wear a Black and Tan medal. Records show that he got a reminder dated 19/07/43 requesting an immediate report of the accident.

When Johnny Gordon retired in 1960, he left behind him his notebook where he detailed some of the court cases he had been involved in. One related to a seizure of a car battery at Carrickcarnan where an individual had been fined £100 for the offence. A more interesting report involving Johnny however, was described in *The Irish News*, Belfast, May 24th 1934, entitled 'Exciting Scene at Border. Customs Officers' Chase after Motorist'. It read: 'Free State and Northern Customs Officers on the border between Newry and Dundalk figured in a very exciting scene yesterday afternoon, which resulted in the arrest of a man and the seizure of a motor-car which is believed to have been stolen. At 5.30 Mr. John Gordon, one of the Free State Customs officials, noticed a motor car being driven from Northern Ireland into the Free State by an unapproved route. The car was coming from a side road at Jonesborough and was being turned onto the main road leading to Dublin at a spot inside the Free State territory when Mr. Gordon signalled to the driver to stop. Instead of doing so he reversed the vehicle on the main road and headed toward Belfast. As he did so Mr. Gordon jumped on his bicycle and followed, waving a paper in his hand and shouting to attract the attention of the Customs officers of both the Free State and Northern Ireland. The huts are in close proximity, and the motorist dashed past but the Free State officers who were on duty rushed out after him. This action resulted in the Northern Ireland officers rushing from their post in time to stop the motorist, who was held up. It later transpired that the man was in possession of an Austin motorcar, which had been stolen from Mr. Elliot, Solicitor, Newry, half an hour earlier. He is believed to be a deserter from the British Army, and he was handed over to the Ulster Constabulary. ' Johnny seems to have been popular with the Northern papers. The *Belfast Telegraph*, May 17th, 1934, reported on Louth Customs cases in which Justice Goff stated he wished to 'very highly commend Customs Officer John Gordon, who had been a witness in a case decided earlier today. ' Johnny's scrapbook ended there. However, the reports give an interesting insight into Customs activity in the earlier days. Just imagine what would be thought of an officer cycling after a car, waving a bit of white paper, at the present time.

Jim, Johnny, Gordon and Francis (Frank) Hayes, Dundalk train station.

In the general office for A.P.O's at the railway station there was a blackboard on the wall where alterations to train times were recorded for our information. On arrival you took note. One member of staff was a regulations man and extra strict. New staff arrivals attracted his attention and he tried to observe how they performed their duties when examining passengers baggage on board the trains. When he attempted to observe me I used the appropriate language which promptly got rid of him. One afternoon when I arrived for duty I saw a great sketch on the blackboard. It was a donkey with our friend's head. The donkey had the station on its back. The subject of the sketch was on night duty but when he saw the sketch he became very angry and said he would report the matter to the revenue commissioners. He even wanted to take the blackboard and offending sketch to Freddie (F. Richardson), the Director of Establishment. Frank Hayes was the artist.

After the pictures one evening, I went into Moloccas in Park Street to have a cup of tea before going back to my digs. As I was drinking my tea, a British custom's official, whom I recognized, came in with two other fellows. They sat down at the table next to me and I could hear the lads talking about the amount of 'stuff' they had on board and that they had to make one further stop down the town, in Bridge Street. I was wondering how I could leave without the customs official spotting me, but when he got up to go to the toilet I slipped out. There were two northern cars outside so I took their numbers and rang Mick Scully at Carrickcarnan frontier post. When they arrived, bottles and cigarettes were discovered in the cars, and when the British Customs official at the frontier post was searched, cheques that the smugglers had paid him with were found. An investigation followed and during that time I was down in Newry when I met the customs official. He called me a so and so, but I walked away without getting into a confrontation. Shortly afterwards the British came down and asked me to make a statement, but I wouldn't. I didn't want to get involved, and maybe have to go to court up north. The next time I was down in Newry I met the customs official again. 'I want to apologise', he said, 'I believe you wouldn't make any statement'. 'That's right', I replied. 'Oh', he said, 'thanks very much'.

In May 1946, an individual appeared before Dundalk District Court on a number of charges, including smuggling. The main charges, however, were related to the attempted bribery of C&E officers Pat Langan and Tommy Woods. The individual involved was fined £200 for each offence. It would seem the smugglers would leave no stone unturned in trying to find this elusive gap and I too was made an offer by a third party of £50 per week if I gave a guarantee that the patrol car would be stationary for one hour at my digs each meal time. I reported the matter to the C.P.O. and we tried to get the identity of the real smuggler behind the attempted bribe but were unsuccessful.

One lad who attended the Training Centre with me was posted to Dublin Port. In the early 1950s he turned up at Carrickcarnan frontier post. Those who worked with him looked on him as an efficient guy and he became secretary of our local branch of the Preventive Staff Association. An election to the Executive Council was due in 1954. There were three places for A.P.Os and he was anxious to go forward for one of the places. There was a series of rumours however and as a result a few influential people did not want this lad to be given the chance so they began looking for an alternative candidate. I was picked and ended up on the Executive Council.

One day I was in the Chief's office when he got a phone call from head office. After the call he asked me where my 'friend' was stationed. I told him but he did not elaborate further. The following morning three inspectors, including J. J O'Doherty arrived at the office and I moved out to the office next door. After some time O'Doherty came out with the keys to the C.P.Os car and asked me to take him to Carrickcarnan frontier post. When we arrived I remained in the car as he made his way in. O'Doherty emerged with our friend in tow. There was little conversation on the return journey to the office. Our friend was escorted into the Chief's office and a very long period of questioning followed. They had reliable evidence of his involvement with a Dublin merchant in smuggling woven tweed for the rag trade. It was alleged that phone tapping was involved. He was suspended that day and later discharged.

The majority of the staff in Dundalk were married. Only Mick Scully, Johnny McMahon and myself were single. When off-duty we had plenty of places to socialize. There were three cinemas, the Adelphi, the Magnet and Park Street. Dancers were well catered for at the Marist Hall, Market House and the Pavilion in Blackrock with Jimmy Hamilton and Dee O'Kane bringing popular bands to the various venues.

One night while at a dance in the Marist Hall a fellow called Dan English introduced himself telling me that his brother Jack had told him to look me up. Jack had served as an officer with me. Dan had started work at the time in the Munster and Leinster Bank now known as the A.I.B. We became friends and he joined our dancing group. We enjoyed his company during a trip to the

I.O.M. Our group also went to dances in Newry and Warrenpoint. One night Benny Walsh, an officer of Customs and Excise in H.M. service, talked us into going to a dance at the Tennis Club on the Glen Road in Belfast. It was a bit careless at the time. Another member of the dancing group was John O'Hare whom I knew from my time in Omeath. The Bachelor's Dance in Newry was the social outing of the year for all dancers. John was taking his girlfriend, Carmel, to their first dress dance and I was glad to accept a lift with them. It was a great night. Carmel and John would eventually marry and we remained lifelong friends.

Menu, The Newry Bachelors, Dance 1950.

A colleague, Sean Gallagher, also an ex-officer in the army, and his wife Ann were expecting a new arrival in the family. Ann's brother and his girlfriend were to be the godparents. There was a problem however and I was asked at short notice to act as proxy godfather. I agreed and met Geenie Murray from Lurgan who was to be the godmother. She visited the Gallaghers regularly and sometime later I saw her at a dance in the Marist Hall. She had a friend, Joan, with her and I was introduced. That was how I met my wife.

Joan lived in Lurgan with her family. Her father, Peter, originally came from the home farm in Balgree Co. Meath. They visited the farm from time to time to see his brother, Tom, who was a bachelor living alone. When Tom died Peter and his wife Ann moved back to Balgree. Joan and her brother, Barry, continued to live at their home in Lurgan. When Joan was travelling to Balgree she would break her journey at Dundalk. We would meet at Maloccas in Park Street and our friendship developed leading to regular visits to Lurgan. The trips to Lurgan included going to the pictures and an odd dance. I was uncomfortable at the pictures as you felt compelled to stand for 'God Save the Queen' before leaving. We decided to give the pictures a miss and go dancing in Banbridge and Portadown. My southern accent did not get a warm welcome in Portadown. We went to Belfast and found it was like Dublin. They had the Saturday afternoon dance just like the Metropole in O'Connell Street in Dublin. Joan's sister was a nurse in the Mater Hospital in Belfast at the time and invited us to their annual dance. We had a great night. I proposed to Joan, she accepted and soon we were on our way to Dublin for the ring. The ring was bought from Fitzpatricks off Grafton Street and the search for a house now began in earnest. We were lucky and had it partially furnished for the big day.

Joan and Jim, 1956.

During this time the I.R.A. carried out an incursion into the Six Counties which became known as the 1950s campaign and coincided with my trips to Lurgan. The 'B Specials' were mobilized. This sectarian force was used to deal with any intruders. They set up patrols everywhere and mobile checkpoints. A southern registered car attracted special attention. To be questioned at the checkpoints was a very unpleasant experience. My marriage to Joan on the 25th September 1957 was to end these trips.

We had four sons, Eugene, Gerry, Peter and Danny. They went on to attend the Friary primary school and did their stint as altar boys before moving to the Marist and third level. We enjoyed seeing them grow up as normal boys and later when they went out into the world we were proud to see them make the most of what was available.

On May 9th 1953, the *Dundalk Democrat* reported on an extraordinary story from Castleblayney about a seized car, containing 71,000 cigarettes and 690 Lbs of creamery butter, which went up in flames damaging shop fronts nearby. Johnny McMahon, who was a pal of mine, and Pat Kelly had seized a V8 car at Oram on June 28th, 1952. They apprehended the driver, Brendan McCauley from Castleblayney, who when stopped, first offered both men £100 each to let him go. Johnny drove the seized car to Castleblayney for examination. McCauley was allowed to accompany him as Kelly drove the patrol car. When they stopped at Muckno Street to pick up the P.O., John King, McMahon got out of the seized car and left McCauley alone in the vehicle for a few short minutes. Suddenly McCauley jumped out, there was a hissing sound, and the car burst into flames. When the fire was put out by the fire brigade John King explained to the court what was found: '...I found Woodbine cigarettes and butter in the back of the car. I saw a 5 gallon drum on top of the goods, the tap was turned on. We removed it, and the goods, from the car and on making a further examination we found a wire from the battery to a switch on the dashboard and a wire leading under the front seat to the wooden box on the floor at the rear, with a second wire from the box to the steering bar. The two wires were connected to two terminals in the box connected with a very fine wire. The drum contained some liquid, which ignited when a light was put to it. I was able to identify 71,000 Woodbines and 690 lbs butter. There was more destroyed that I could not estimate. The Woodbines were not usable but some of the butter was sold for a small price'. John King valued the cigarettes at £310.12.06 and the butter at £103.10.00 and the penalty sought was three times that amount, £1242.7.6. Frank Roe, defending, suggested; 'there were 101 ways in which a fire might start'. Johnny McMahon was lucky he wasn't burned alive. Seemingly, the smugglers involved, were determined that, if caught, the evidence could be destroyed to prevent the Customs getting their hands on it. The bomb, for that's what it was, may have been crude, but it proved highly effective as McCauley was able to ignite it in seconds. The judge, Mr. Kenny, had no doubt about the guilt of McCauley and fined him £1242.07.06 on the charge of attempting to bring goods to a place for exportation, and £10 on the charge of attempting to destroy the goods. He didn't pay the fine and did 6 months in Mountjoy jail.

Sometime during mid-1955 the phone rang in the office. It was a message from Headquarters with news that John Gerard Walsh had passed the C.P.O's exam. I rang him at Carrickcarnan with the good news. Years later, in 1968, while I was on duty at Carrickcarnan, he was able to reciprocate, calling from the C.P.Os office in St Patricks Hall to give me the news that I had also made C.P.O.

Customs & Excise Preventive Staff Association's annual general meeting at the St Lawrence Hotel, Howth.
Front: Messrs R. O Cinnsealaigh, editor 'the Customs Journal'; D. Crowley, Secretary; J. Burns, President; K. O'Dowda, General Treasurer; P.O Morain, member of council.
Back: T Mac Carthaigh, member and Chairman of Revenue Staff Panel; J. O'Shea, member of Staff Panel; S. O Ploingcead, do.; B. Donnelly, do. and R.N. Halliday,

P.S.A. Executive Council & Officers, 1954-55
J. Brennan, D. A. Crowley, T. McGushin, K. O'Dowda, R.S. O
Cinnsealaigh, T. MacCarthaigh, J. O'Shea, S. O Ploingcead,
R.N. Halliday (Staff panel representative), J.J. Burns, B.J. Donnelly,
P. O Morain
Courtesy *Irish Independant.*

In 1956 there was an interview for promotion to officer announced. All of us applied but I was not called. When the interviews had concluded the rumour was that Tom McCarthy and Donal Crowley had been successful. One morning soon after though the phone rang, it was the Collector. He informed me that I was for interview at 3 p.m. that afternoon at Dublin Castle and explained that it was in my interest to attend. He instructed me to inform the C.P.O. that if there was not a suitable train available for the journey that the C.P.O. was to provide a mobile car to take me to Dublin. Travelling by train I arrived at the Castle expecting to see some more candidates however I seemed to be the only one present. Soon the door opened and Donal Mulcahy emerged. We had only exchanged greetings when I was called in for the interview. I had a funny feeling about the situation and didn't take it too seriously. Afterwards I discovered that my suspicions had been correct and 'I was not at the races'. Donal Mulcahy and Andy Desmond had been promoted. This provided me with plenty to think about. During the same year Joe McGee retired. He was a big loss and was given a great send off. The creation of mobile patrols was his most important legacy. After some time John Gerard Walsh became his successor.

In 1958 we got our own Inspector General in the person of Mr J.P. O'Reilly, late surveyor of the Special investigation Branch He was also a barrister and was known as the judge. A very pompous individual, he arrived in Dundalk to visit the stations with John Gerard. On return to the office the C.P.O. told me that he had a funny incident to tell. They had arrived at Drumbilla frontier post to find Jimmy Agnew A.P.O. (an ex 4th Northern man) standing nearby when he should have been on foot patrol at Ballsmill un-approved road. Jimmy was in the act of lighting his pipe as the judge commenced to lecture him. John Gerard was amazed to see Jimmy calmly continue to puff away on his pipe, despite the lecture which was obviously having no effect. The judge was taken down a peg or two.

I was promoted to P.O. on 21/10/1960 and directed to travel to Monaghan to replace Kevin O'Dowda who was on sick leave commencing on 22/10/1960. Kevin was a brother of Brendan O'Dowda, the well known singer. We had a patrol car and a frontier post at Tyholland. I got good digs and enjoyed the work. Around this time my aunt Mollie bought me my first car, a second hand V.W. Beetle Reg no WI.5168, from Walsh's Garage in Thomastown. As I had just been promoted the timing of the purchase was perfect as I was constantly on the move doing relief duties. With a salary of £440 a year, buying a car myself was still beyond my reach. Joan and I tried to repay her in some little way by having her visit us. aunt Mollie got on well with Joan who took her to see the sites north and south. After Monaghan I worked at a number of stations including Swanlibar, Clones, Dublin and Carrickarnan.

While at Dublin I worked with a sanctimonious P.O. called Willy John. A self-righteous character, he had a particular dislike for the adult literature that could sometimes be encountered on some of the foreign ships saying it was 'not fit for Irish eyes'. A story goes that while on duty one night at 47, City Quay, which was on the south side of the river, he had sent his two A.P.O's out on patrol and was taking a snooze in their absence. This, apparently, was common practice for Willy John. The C.P.O, however, had decided to pay him a visit that same night. On entering the office, the C.P.O. came upon the curious scene of Willy John asleep, but rather than wake the P.O. he quietly tip-toed around him, signed the book and exited, making his way down to the two A.P.Os who were out patrolling the quayside. 'Don't tell Willy John I was around' the C.P.O. instructed the two lads. Barely able to contain themselves, the two lads made their way back to the office to the now awake Willy John. 'Well had the C.P.O. anything to say?' said one lad with a smirk to Willy John. 'No, why?' he replied. 'We were talking to him down on the quay there'. A quick glance at the book and the C.P.O's signature in it confirmed the visit much to Willy John's embarrassment.

While I was on boarding duties a Norwegian ship came in to port. When it was tied up and the gangway in place we boarded. Boarding duties entailed locking and 'sealing' the bonded store on board the ship which meant the seal could not be broken without Customs permission while the ship was in port. The captain, who had good English, had never been in Ireland before and had not issued his crew of 8 its allowance of 1 bottle and 200 cigarettes for use. I permitted him to take the bulk issue and distribute it later which made it possible for me to secure and seal the bonded store. Willy John and his rummage crew, which the captain referred to as 'the black gang', were on the quayside waiting for me to finish before coming on board. I noticed that, in common with most foreign ships, a selection of mild pornography was on display, strewn across the tables. I told the Captain to give Willy John a cup of coffee and a few magazines when he got there to keep him happy and then went about my business, boarding another ship further along the quayside.

About an hour afterwards I was coming back up the quayside and there was the Norwegian captain on the deck looking extremely irate and shaking his fist at me. I guessed Willy John didn't like the coffee. Quoting regulations, Willy John had a dig at me afterwards about not adhering to the rules regarding the issuing of the crew's ration. I explained that the rules were guidelines only and I was simply speeding up the process and thought he'd understand.

Carrickcarnan

In 1962 I was sent on temporary duty to Carrickcarnan frontier post, between Dundalk and Newry on the main Belfast to Dublin road. It was the premier frontier post in the country but, at the time, the buildings for the Preventive staff were very primitive, just tin sheds with dry toilets.

While travelling to some function in Armagh, the then Minister for Finance, Mr McEntee stopped at the post and asked if he could use the toilet. I took him round the back to the dry toilet and informed him that this was all that was available. 'Oh', he said, 'this is bad'. I informed him that there were plans to build a new frontier post and suggested that he might use his good offices and give it a push.

In 1963 Pat Carroll retired as a P.O. and I got the opportunity to fill the vacancy in Omeath starting on 08/05/1963. Omeath was a changed place. The railway was no more but the ferries were still operating even though the numbers travelling were now very small. There was very little happening in Omeath at that time with only the pirate radio station m/v Radio Caroline, which was fitted out at Greenore, providing the locals with a little bit of excitement.

We had a completely new staff and Pat had been given the choice to continue serving as an A.P.O. as his service did not give him a full pension. Our roles were reversed as I was now the boss. The official car had been withdrawn which didn't help and I was forced to use my own car to do the visits to Carlingford and Greenore. Covering sanction however, for using my own car for official duties, was slow in coming. One day Superintendent P. Denver arrived on inspection and I used the opportunity to raise the covering sanction issue with him. Indifferent to my plight he told me that better men had 'cycled' and did the job. I informed him that I was not going to cycle even though he might have done it in the past and suffered when, after the change in government in 1932, consequent to the reduction in the cost of bicycles at the time, the allowance for use on official business had been reduced from 2 Shillings 6 pence to 2 Shillings from 01/01/1933 (Circular E389).

In spite of adversity I carried on and two years later in August 1965, I was appointed to the 'new' frontier post at Carrickcarnan.

9 | THE ASSOCIATION

When I went back to Carrickcarnan the Board of Works had built the new frontier post. However, they had built it to their own specifications, not to the Customs specifications. To be fair it was a nice building, but its position was completely wrong. It was built on one side of the road, whereas to be fully effective you needed to have traffic going on each side of you. Eventually they did build another structure on the other side of the road to deal with exports.

One day the Inspector General arrived and announced, 'This is the premier frontier post in the country. I want all the staff to be in full uniform all the time, particularly when on duty out on the road'. Now, our Staff Association had been seeking proper uniforms for years, and an allowance to enable us to buy shirts. In light of this the Inspector General's announcement really rankled with us, so we devised a plan to highlight our demands.

We had a photograph taken of one of the staff in full uniform, minus his shirt and collar, tie and boots, and his face obscured. We published the photograph in the next issue of our *customs journal*. It brought our problem to the forefront and helped to achieve much needed progress surrounding the whole uniform issue.

In 1964 the Association began to prepare a salary claim for all three grades. Garret Fitzgerald was commissioned to get the claim ready for presentation to the official side. Tom McCarthy and Donal Crowley were the staff negotiators. Numerous meetings took place and ended in October 1965 when a reasonable offer was on the table at conciliation. Garret recommended acceptance as did the executive. The general body of staff however forced a referendum and rejected the offer. Arbitration was the

Customs Journal Uniform.

next step and Tom and Donal had to take on the task.

In 1966 the arbitrator's award was published. The outcome was a disaster. In his judgement Mr. Cook S.C. chairman saw fit to award much less than what had been rejected at conciliation. The loss was considerable with A.P.O.s losing £85 at the minimum salary and £110 at the maximum salary. P.O's and C.P.O.s lost £155 at the minimum salary and £185 at the maximum salary. There was unanimous dismay and disgust at the outcome. Every branch in the country was calling for action with varying degrees of militancy being expressed. It was during this time I was elected as P.O. representative on the executive of the Preventive Staff association and at the same time was appointed its president. This was the climate that greeted me within weeks of becoming president of the P.S.A., a position I held for the next six years. (For full Executive Team, see appendices)

Association matters took up a lot of my time. The views expressed at branch meetings all over the country became known at the Inspector General's office. This resulted in frequent contact with his highness. He constantly referred to Carrickarnon as the premier frontier post in the country and expected very high standards from all staff. He tried to persuade me to rent the official house at Carrickcarnon saying that any newly married woman should be delighted with a new house. The location was not suitable I said and reminded him that the frontier post was the first stop for drunken day trippers when buses discharged them to off-load.

John Domoney, the second P.O. at the frontier post, was glad to take the house. Our scheme of attendance was 8 a.m. – 4 p.m. and 4 p.m.-midnight. John was a great cook and often served a nice lunch. He was strict on regulations however, having spent sometime in the Training Centre as an instructor.

We had an unannounced visit from Mr. P. Denver, Preventive Superintendant. He expressed a special interest in the record of statistics kept. The staff referred to this record as the 'handball book' in which they entered the number of vehicles crossing at the frontier post. No instructions had been given on how the count was to be taken. Denver came up with the novel idea that the A.P.O. on duty on the road would keep ten small marbles in his pocket and transfer them to the other pocket each time a car passed. In the end he didn't issue any marbles so the lads were left with stones in their pockets instead.

The traffic at the frontier post was very heavy and there was some congestion at times. We had a very welcome visitor to the Frontier Post one day, the county engineer Mr. Liam Bruen. After a suggestion Mr Bruen agreed to widen the road, as he had some money left over in his budget, which gave some relief from the congestion. On another occasion Mr Bruen made a repeat visit to the frontier post and explained that that due to the continued high volume of traffic passing through Dundalk, the Council wanted a record of the cross border section, and proposed a traffic counting device be put in place and asked that we take the readings. We gladly accepted on agreement that he would replace or repair any broken or damaged cables during the process. Accurate statistics were now available for the first time and so the short lived 'stones in the pockets' system was relegated to history.

The judge was correct when he described Carrickcarnan as the premier frontier post in the country. The sheer volume of private and commercial traffic kept us very busy. Everyday something new happened giving rise to problems. The application of common sense helped to achieve quick solutions most of the time and the Rules and Regulations were used as guides.

The Department of Transport & Power issued licences to hauliers from the U.K. and N.I. to enable them to carry goods in the State. Sometimes however, one would arrive at the station without the licence. Usually a phone call to the Department would result in the issue of the license and its number for endorsement on the documents. On Saturdays the Department was not available to deal with the offending haulier. One Saturday due to the urgency of the merchandise I allowed the load to proceed minus the license. It was subsequently picked up in Drogheda by the Traffic Corps. I had to explain my decision to the Department. The next Saturday I was faced with a similar problem, I held up the load. There was intense pressure coming from Customs Clearance and the driver to have the load cleared. After some time I suggested to the C.C. boss Paddy Beagan, to ask Mr

McArdle, C.I.E. manager to provide a unit to replace the British registered unit. The C.I.E unit eventually hooked up to the load and delivered the merchandise.

After one of my many meetings in Dublin Castle, Commissioner Culligan asked me to stay behind. He asked me how I got on with the Customs Clearance Company. I told him that they gave a good service to the public but that sometimes they expected the impossible. Apparently an individual got an interview with the commissioner to complain about the service he received from Customs. His main complaints were directed at the road station but he also mentioned my name and the incident about the lorry. The Commissioner said the he had no cause for complaint and that I had actually solved his problem. I was the white haired boy ever after with Paddy Beagan.

I was on duty when Dr. T.K. Whitaker came to meet Terence O'Neill, Prime Minister of Northern Ireland on his return visit to meet Sean Lamass. It was a historic day. We had a number of prominent people as frequent visitors including Brian Faulkner and Sir George Clarke, Grand Master of the Orange lodge. Sir George attended race meetings and gave many a winner to the staff. One day I saw Todd Andrews, he served on a number of government boards standing on the road. Todd had been the driving force behind Bord na Mona and had the ear of Sean Lamass. I greeted him and asked if I could help. He asked how I knew him and I informed him that he had interviewed me years before for a job in Bord na Mona. Apparently he never owned a motor car himself as in the past a car went with the job and needed assistance with a pass. I got him fixed up and over a cup of tea we had a chat while the job was processed. When the stamping of Customs passes for motor vehicles was abolished in 1974 it helped to speed up the traffic.

An undercurrent of unease was widespread attributable to the arbitrator award. A new salary claim was out so it was decided to seek clerical officer status for A.P.O's. Pat Moran, Rory Murphy and Sean Plunkett played an important role in compiling the 32-page claim. It was presented to Liam Morrissey, Director of Establishment, who was chairman of the Conciliation Board. Meetings were held at regular intervals but the dialogue became repetitive and little progress was made. We heard Morrissey's promise 'let me judge when the climate is right to go to finance' ad nauseam.

I attended the annual meeting of the T.U.C. in Portrush where I met Maurice Cosgrave, secretary of the Postal Workers Union. During my period at the Curragh Maurice was a clerical officer at the Post Office. We met socially. Harold O'Sullivan of the Local Government Officials Union was seeking election to the executive of the T.U.C. Maurice asked me to vote for Harold which I gladly did. Harold was an ex-army officer that I met in 1943. He was glad to be elected. Both he and Maurice promised to give us all the help they could. They were experienced negotiators. Maurice invited me to his office in Parnell Square telling me to call if I needed help. The invitation was extended to members of the executive.

In many ways the Preventive staff were innocents abroad. I took a Dale Carnegie course in the Derryhale Hotel in Dundalk. Dale Carnegie's main objective was to teach people 'how to win friends and influence people'. In my case, I took it in an effort to improve my debating skills. The course included a number of solicitors and business men. We had plenty of debates that helped improve the gift of being able to think on your feet.

We had a number of informal meetings with 'the judge'. Sean Plunkett and myself were at one of these meetings when Commissioner Culligan was present. The judge went on the attack telling me that he was fed up with all my complaints and listed some small improvements in promotion etc. It would appear that the idea behind this meeting was to let the Commissioner see that he was standing up to the Association and their demands. When I got a chance to reply I acknowledged the improvements but that I was there to talk about what he hadn't done. Mobile patrols was an issue that left him and the Commissioner vulnerable. I informed him that we had mobile patrols working irregular hours and exposing themselves to abuse and inclement weather, and their efforts are not being fairly rewarded. They were providing a service to the Revenue that they were not being paid for. I explained that we were simply seeking the same allowances that the British Customs had in Northern Ireland and asked them to look across the border at the Waterguard, I was very proud of the mobile staff and that they deserved better treatment.

The meeting was adjourned.

Mr J.P. O'Reilly
"The judge".

Commissioner Culligan.

Afterwards Commissioner Culligan called for another meeting that afternoon at which an agreed report was reached to pay the mobile patrols an allowance of 10 hours overtime per week. The copy of the agreed report giving effect to the allowance is dated the 22nd of June '67, back-dated to the 6th of May '67, the day of our meeting at Dublin Castle. The success with the mobile allowance affected only a small number of staff but it was generally welcomed.

It represented a small step forward and eased the militancy amongst the Preventive staff. The negotiation of the A.P.O. status claim continued however, as did the frequent meetings with the judge, often one to one at the Inspector General's office, which was on Lord Edward Street near the Castle. In the course of visiting the Castle I met the judge one day and he began talking about some problem. He remarked that 'this would have to happen as this was the 20th Century', I agreed but I said if it's the 20th century here in Dublin it's also the 20th Century in Omeath referring to my own driving claim. He said he'd get it fixed up for me. True to his word I was back in Carrickarnan when I got paid but Mr. P. Denver, Preventive Superintendent, had restricted the number of claims and so I didn't get reimbursed for the full number of visits I had made.

While at Carrickcarnan, the same Denver arrived in around midnight one night. He said to me 'Jim, I'm not doing an official visit, but put his name in the book all the same. 'If I wasn't here would it be official?' I replied. 'Jim' he said, 'If you go on the way you're going, you'll injure your promotional prospects'. I asked him if he or the Revenue Commissioners were not satisfied with the way I was performing my duties. He eased off. I seemed to have a run in with him every time he appeared around the place.

On another occasion Seamus Coyle had discovered a large quantity of various goods in a container that had been reported empty. We could not, however, list the goods in the 40ft container without unloading the lot. I consulted the C.P.O. for guidance due to the people involved. He got in touch with head office in Dublin and subsequently P. Denver rang me demanding a list of goods so that he could give a decision. I explained that this was not possible. Taking the easy way out, he instructed me to release the goods for immediate exportation on payment of a £100 penalty. Some of the lads had contacted the British Customs in the meantime however, and the container was duly seized as it made its way back across the Border.

It was obvious that the Revenue Commissioner knew very little about the Preventive staff except what he had heard from others. After throwing the notion around, it was suggested that we invite him down to a dinner dance which would provide an ideal opportunity for the Commissioner to better acquaint himself with our staff. Paul McNeill had been involved with some of the dinner dances in Dublin and so himself and a few others set about organizing the event. We issued the invitation to Commissioner Culligan and his wife and they came down. Delighted with the evening, he was particularly impressed with the lads and their reaction to his presence. It was a point in our favour. In 1969, Commissioner Culligan attended a meeting with Dundalk Chamber of Commerce at the Ballymac Hotel. He used the opportunity to pay an impromptu visit to our offices at St Patricks Hall. I was on leave at the time but he had a great chat with John Lynch. They discussed fishing and John identified some trout fishing rivers for him. The next time I spoke with the Commissioner he expressed a clear vote of confidence in my judgement by stating I could contact him directly if necessary.

While attending the Chamber of Commerce meeting at the Ballymascanlon Hotel, Commissioner Culligan was brought up to date on how smuggling and roadside markets damaged legitimate trade. Members of the travelling community were involved. When caught they willingly paid hefty deposits to have their vans released and the goods seized. We realized that there was big money being made and a decision was made to seize both the vehicles and goods. The result was that the office was mobbed by women and groups of young children looking for the return of the seized vans claiming the children had nowhere else to sleep. I explained that I could not help as the order had come from Dublin Castle. They landed up in the Castle and I had a phone call from John O'Flynn, principal of Division 2, blaming me for having his tranquility so rudely shattered. I pleaded not guilty and we remained friends.

Meanwhile our negotiations continued in the background and the news on the grapevine was that Morrissey was stone walling our claim. Our friends in the T.U.C. knew the problems and suggested that an approach to the Minister of Finance was our only option. We had no friends in high places that could oblige. For civil servants it would be breaking all the rules. All possibilities were investigated and eventually the Minister was made aware of the situation and agreed to meet us. Our next meeting with Morrissey proved the grapevine correct. Morrissey's final answer to us was 'It's not on'. He was quickly informed that we were not prepared to accept this as an answer to the 32-page claim and two years of dialogue. The voice of militancy could be heard loud and clear amongst the numbers. Soon after though, the Judge retired and was replaced by one of our own, Cormac Kilty, who was sympathetic to our claim.

The militant groups within our association booked Liberty Hall for a meeting at which it was intended to get approval for strike action. We were called to a meeting with the official side the day before Liberty Hall. Commissioner Culligan was chairman. In attendance were the Superintendant Inspector, the Inspector General and L. Morrissey the Director of Establishments. Withdrawal of labour was the main topic.

The Commissioner spoke at length to explain that he could not allow the traffic to be held up in the absence of staff and would have to let it move without interference. We explained that it was not that simple. I suggested that he should listen to our side rather than to Mr. Morrissey. Sean Plunkett informed the official side that we were affiliated to the T.U.C. and given the required notice, the strike would be official. This meant that trade unionists would not pass the picket and nothing would be moving which would have serious consequences for the country. We would be very reluctant to go down that road but the official side was pushing us in that direction. We did not want to be the first Revenue staff to take strike action.

The continuing discussion allowed us to emphasize our predicament. We informed them that if a solution was not found today we would be meeting the Minister. There was silence in the room, then the Commissioner turned to me. 'Can we meet at eleven o'clock in the morning?' I asked him how it would be possible to have an offer in the morning if they could not make us one tonight. 'I'll go to the Minister tonight' he said.

We met at the Castle the following morning to be told by Commissioner Culligan that the Minister had agreed that A.P.O.s would be granted clerical officer status. He is alleged to have asked what century they thought they were in. Before we left Morrissey invited me in to his office saying that I should write a letter thanking the Minister. My reply was that I would do that in my own time. On reflection, however, I agreed and the letter was typed and sent. The letter was received and an acknowledgment sent back to me a short time afterwards. During our chat Morrissey mentioned that Haughey was a good friend to the Civil Service. He introduced pensions for widows of civil servants and made it retrospective.

Liberty Hall was next so it was necessary to keep under cover. The nearby Clarence Hotel was ideal for this purpose. We had a meal to celebrate, and afterwards I decided that the victory deserved a cigar and Irish Coffee. We then went over to Liberty Hall where assembled members from all over the country gave the news that our claim had been successful a wonderful rousing reception. Pat Moran, Sean Plunkett and myself on that night thought back to 1954/55 when clerical officer status for A.P.O.s was first discussed at the executive. It begged the question, why did it take so long?

I met Tom McCarthy, Preventive superintendent at Head Office on Lord Edward Street a few days later. The Inspector General, Cormac Kilty had told him that he was proud of the Preventive staff following the way we behaved at the meeting.

The work of the Revenue protection continued. Much to my surprise, a year or so later, when the next promotion round came up I was promoted to CPO – Chief Preventive Officer. During my period as C.P.O. at Head Office, Cormac Kilty asked me what place I thought the judge had given me in his recommendation for the C.P.O.s exam. I said I had no idea but I didn't think it would be too high. I was surprised when Cormac showed me in first place.

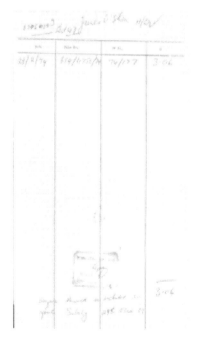

C & E discussion group
4th November 1954.

Seizure reward 1979.

10 | RETURN TO DUNDALK

In Nov. 1968 I was appointed to Chief Preventive Officer and did the rounds for a while, here there and everywhere. Some time was spent at Head Office in Dublin, then in Ballyshannon, Co. Donegal, Dublin Airport and Dublin Port. I was then put in charge of mobile patrols in Dundalk and Monaghan, and was based in the latter but as most of the smuggling activity was in Dundalk I had to travel there every day.

Naturally 'the Troubles' caused problems. The main Dundalk/ Newry road was a regular target. Both real and hoax bombs were frequently used to block the road making it impassable for merchandise. As a result, safe alternative routes had to be found for imports and exports. On one occasion a colleague was stopped one morning while driving to work by a group who claimed to be I.R.A. They removed him from his car and took him into the fields close to the salient road. Two men remained with him. After about an hour he heard an explosion and was told by the two men 'that was your car' before they left him. My brush with the I.R.A. happened one morning when I was called to the office at 2 a.m. A patrol had detained a resident from Northern Ireland with a van load of goods. He was claiming special treatment as a member of the I.R.A. We informed him that we carried out our duties in a uniform manner and that there was no provision for special treatment for any group. It took some time for him to accept his position but when he realised that we would be seizing the van his mood changed. I eventually offered to release the van for £100. He enquired where I thought he'd get the money from. We reminded him that if he was who he claimed to be he would have no trouble getting it. He arrived back with the money and the van was released. As I walked with him out of the office he produced a revolver, claiming that he didn't have to surrender if he had decided otherwise. The gun was then put away and the individual went on his way. As a general rule we adopted the 'see nothing, hear nothing and say nothing' attitude to matters outside carrying out of our duties.

In April 1969, they changed the C.P.O.s Office from Monaghan to Dundalk and so I moved back to Dundalk on a permanent basis and made St Patrick's Hall my new home. One of the first things I noticed was the aerial for our base radio control station

OIFIG AN AIRE AIRGEADAIS
(OFFICE OF THE MINISTER FOR FINANCE)
BAILE ÁTHA CLIATH 2
(DUBLIN 2)

7 August 1969

Mr James O'Shea
President
Customs & Excise Preventive
Staff Association

Dear Mr O'Shea

I am much obliged for your letter of 11 July 1969, conveying your personal thanks and also the thanks of your Association in regard to recent matters affecting the Preventive Services.

Yours sincerely

Charles J Haughey

Acknowledgement from
Minister, Charles J Haughey.

lying on top of a press. The O.P.W. arranged to have it erected on the roof which resulted in greater range and a clearer signal for our communications. While doing some exercises with the new range of radio communication we had two good seizures of pigs from the same client a few days apart. He arrived at the office afterwards asking did I want to 'put out his smoke altogether' ?

The Seizure in the Bay - November 1969

Dennis Farren, the C.P.O.s clerk brought me up to date with the rumours regarding the smuggling at the Port. Forgeign registered vessels with their cargo of Polish coal from Gdansk were the natural suspects. Certain pubs in the town were alleged to to secure regular supplies of spirits and cigarettes from this traffic. Gdansk was behind the Iron Curtain which ruled out any chance of information.

The M/V *Marie Both*, a Dutch registerd ship was mentioned as one of the suppliers. We arranged to have special rummage crews ready for her next arrival. I was present when the rummage commenced, but I got a message to return to my office as the Inspector General wanted to see me. His view was that we would not get much in a cargo of coal.

On my return to the quay, the harbour master informed me that the dockers had stoppped work. They didn't like the Customs snoopping around, so they downed tools. Raymond Watters, the main union offical arrived and asked what could be done. I tock him over to the Custom House and showed him "Highmoores" book on customs laws. He asked for a loan of the book and went to address the strikers. He read the relevant section loud and clear and ended saying " this is the f-ing law of the land" so you better get back to work. They did as they were told.

The rummage delivered a good seizure, 4,000 cigarettes and 500 gallons of spirit. Dennis said, he thought it was the tip of the iceberg.

We decided to give more attention to the traffic in the port and identified the ships coming from Gdansk. The M/V *Friedel*, a German ship, was picked for special attention on her next trip. We had staff in position on both sides of the bay. The ship was in their view as she sailed towards the harbour and they observed the activity with the pilot boat.

In the office, Dennis and myself could hear over the radio, a running commentary on what was taking place in the bay. Goods were off loaded onto the pilot boat and it made for the Blue Anchor. The pilot boat turned back into the bay and transferred the goods onto another open boat anchored at sea. The staff sounded helpless from the comments over the radio.

Liam Ó Gogain P.O. and Bernard White A.P.O. came to the office and explained the position. It looked like a very big load they said and begged me to get a boat somewhere.

Customs and Excise had no boat however. Here we were, a service with the 'boatman' tag given to us by the controlling grade, without a boat. There were very few owners of small boats that could be approached. One guy who serviced the buoys in the harbour was our choice. We found him in a pub and eventually talked him into taking us to check out a boat that was interfering with normal traffic. When we were afloat I explained to him that there might be some stuff on board. He replied 'in that case you better take the tiller'. This brought me back to my youth on the River Barrow. My two colleagues were wearing uniform heavy coats and caps. I was not dressed for the occasion however and had no protection against the November weather but the excitement kept me going. As we moved out into the bay, we could see the boat being towed in the direction of the Ballymascanlon estuary. We made the interception before it made land and seized the boat and its contents. In an effort to protect the owner of our boat, I quoted the Customs Act and informed him that he was still obliged to give assistance. We took the loaded boat in tow and made our way back to the quay side. When we unloaded the cargo we discovered almost a million cigarettes of various brands. We had so many cigarettes piled up on the dockside that it looked like a small house! We then transferred the cigarettes to the office.

In the meantime Mick Crowley went on board the *Friedel* and took its captain, Garber, back to the office. When I returned I brought the captain to the lock up where I showed him the goods we had found. 'That much' ? he said. He then looked for sympathy, saying that he would have to sell his house to get the money for the fine he was likely to receive. We suspected it wasn't his first time, so he got no sympathy from us and Mick Crowley charged him. Later that evening we took the smuggled goods to the State warehouse in Dublin. The Inspector General and his second in command, Mick Scully, were waiting for us. They offered us their congratulations and even bought us a drink! The seizure was the biggest seizure in the history of the British Isles.

The boat was held until the court had given its judgement and on a visit to the captain we discovered that he was celebrating his birthday so, as a consolation, I brought him down a cigar! Captain Garber of the *Friedel* was subsequently convicted and fined £10,000. Once he paid the fine his boat was released and he was escorted out of the harbour by a pilot boat. We received congratulations all round. It was the largest seizure of cigarettes at sea in these islands. For some reason, however, Head Office told us to treat it as 'a once off' seizure and to concentrate on the border. Duly noted, we watched both the border and the sea and made plenty of seizures as a result. One such seizure involved the M/V *Merlin* on which over one million assorted cigarettes were discovered as well as 60 cases of brandy and whiskey. We had another big seizure that was taken ashore and deposited in the boat house at the Soldiers Point. We were supprised at the size of the seizures. It took some organisation to distribute that quantity of cigarettes and spirits. This group had identified a very lucrative market and were determined to continue.

The supply line consisted of the the ships captains who would purchase the goods in Gdansk and would get paid when they were delivered. Non-delivery caused a problem for these captains as the number of large seizures increased over the next few years. The supply line needed to be overhauled and the search was on for an alternative method. A very adventurous undertaking was introduced by the smugglers who would rendezvous with a "passing ship" on the open seas at a pre-determined time and place. This proved to be problematic for the smugglers. Eventually, the traffic developed to a scale we could not have imagined in our wildest dreams.

The seizures kept coming in and Sean Plunkett, now a C.P.O, was sent to Dundalk to help deal with the ever increasing volume of work.

11 | London 1969

In 1969 I went to Kingsbeam House in London for a ten-day seminar. It was the practice, that on promotion to CPO, there were conferences to be attended across the water. Normally two people would go but I was sent on my own to participate in general discussions regarding Customs and Excise, including exchanging information and views. One topic of conversation there was the seizure in Dundalk Bay of one million cigarettes. They were surprised with the methods we used to seize that amount of cigarettes, without a proper boat and crew, having sold our last two boats at Moville back in 1923. We also had a wide-ranging discussion on the duty-free setup for passengers. Duty-free was in existence between the U.K. and France but not with the Republic of Ireland. I raised the question and was informed by a lady Revenue Commissioner that it was simply an arrangement between the two administrations. This news became a very interesting topic of conversation. Mr Heffernan of Aer Lingus informed me that both B & I and Aer Lingus would take the matter up with the relevant authorities. Soon after duty-free was introduced and, over time, it proved to be extremely lucrative for both companies as they went on to make good profits from their sales.

It wasn't always plain sailing on the Association front. There was a controversial matter of a scheme of attendance for discussion at one of our meetings. There were two strong personalities on opposite sides of the debate compounding the matter. I considered that they were both friends of mine. With no sign of a compromise, my lack of action was interpreted as taking one side, that of Sean Plunkett's. The matter got extensive airing in the Customs *Journal*. I declined to use the pages of the Journal and prolonged the argument and incurred the displeasure of a section of the Dublin staff due to my controversial decision.

The existing arrangement had been established in 1953 which saw me taken into the C.P.O.s office from the mobile patrol at a loss of ten hours overtime. The loss was made up by attendances at Dundalk Rail. Instructors at the Training Centre were recompensed by attendance at Dublin Airport. It may not have been the ideal solution.

In 1970 I joined a local Dundalk Art Group and began painting. It proved to be an extremely interesting and enjoyable form of relaxation and was a welcome distraction from my jobs in both the Revenue and the P.S.A. Years later I had become competent enough to present Commissioner Culligan with one of my painting to mark his retirement in 1974.

Re-organisation and Re-training

Decimalization took place in 1971. We remembered De Gaulle's veto in 1963 against Ireland's entry to the E.E.C. Now, however, our entry seemed to be on the horizon. Commissioner Culligan had been Chairman of the Customs Co-operative Council from 1967 until he became Commissioner in 1969 and made a big impression in Europe.

Revenue decided to reorganize in anticipation of our entry and the usual formal and informal meetings began. Comhaltas Cana appeared to be taking a 'not an inch'! attitude from the start. At a meeting, its president, Liam Kennedy, told me that he would not have 'an ex-boatman' supervising his members. I thought it was a last pathetic insult from the past heralding the demise of the poor old boatman tag. Liam eventually handed over to Brian Power and a few more reasonable members of Comhaltas. Both sides were now able to agree the terms of the reorganization of the Customs service.

In March 1974, I was promoted as a surveyor and taken in for retraining. Part of my retraining was done at the Guinness brewery. The staff involved were Andy Desmond, who was a surveyor, and an officer called Clayton Jones. We got on well. Andy had been one of two A.P.O.s first promoted back in 1956 and was father to Dermot Desmond of Financial Services Centre fame. Donal Mulcahy was the second. Both went on to become inspectors and collectors proving that members of the Preventive staff could perform if given the chance. After this breakthrough however, there was only a trickle of promotions over the years until re-organisation eventually took place.

I did the rounds in Dublin Airport and Headquarters for a time and while on duty one day as a surveyor at Dublin Airport I saw a well known smuggler and had a few words with him. I remarked to Paddy O Sullivan, a collector visiting at the time, that the guy I spoke to must be a millionaire by now from all his smuggling. The comment seemed to surprise the Collector who asked me how I knew him. Years later in Dundalk, this collector would attempt to make life difficult by interfering in the running of my station. On another occasion during my time at the Airport, a collector named Mr Eugene O'Mahony, asked me to tackle a very sensitive problem. It took some time but was finished to his satisfaction. Fulsome in his praise, he asked me to call to his office where he produced some cigars and a wee glass in celebration.

In June 1976 I was appointed as the surveyor in charge of the Dundalk No. 1 district, which included the railway station, the port, the frontier post and the mobile patrols. *Iris Leabhar* (the journal published by the Landing Staff association) overflowed with unfavourable comment about my promotion which begged the question, what were they afraid of? The precedent was already established. The reception I received varied from station to station but luckily I had a sense of humur and continued doing my job in spite of the criticism.

My wife Joan was fully behind me during this difficult period. Her only comment was that she hoped something worthwhile would come out of it all. One day I received a query from the collector, Paddy O Sullivan. It was headed 'For the Information of the Revenue Commissioners'. The subject of the query was that I had neglected to have regard for economy in the running of my district. The fact that I allowed an officer to claim subsistence illegally was the alleged offence. It gave me great pleasure to quote, on the reverse side of the query, the circumstances that validated the claim. Sometime later, while in the Customs House, Aidan McNamara the indoor collector called me in and asked me what was I trying to do to poor O'Sullivan. I replied that it was not what I was trying to do to him but rather what he was trying to do to me. Aidan stated that he had seen the query and that I wouldn't be hearing anything more on the matter.

I'd been happy at my job for years but the job satisfaction was now absent in this new set up. I checked with the Revenue

Commissioners regarding the credit owed for my army service and found that I could retire on full pension after July 1982. Mick Scully, a good friend of mine who had been promoted to inspector, also expressed his dissatisfaction with the job and when he told me he was doing a pre-retirement course I arranged to do it also. We both attended the course, which was held in the Buswell's Hotel on Molesworth Street in Dublin. During this time I was involved in a high-level investigation and felt I had to see it to its conclusion before retiring. The fact that it was successful in the end made me feel happy that I had been active in Revenue Protection right up until the eve of my retirement on the 12th July 1985, when both myself and Mick Scully retired together.

Some years after I had retired I joined Gerry McGeough for a coffee in the Imperial Hotel in Dundalk. He was interested in discussing two particular seizures. He began talking about the first which had taken place way back in 1951. He proceeded to tell me that he knew who had informed. I told him that I didn't know who was responsible but that if I did I wouldn't tell him anyway. He repeated that he knew who received the information but incorrectly referred to an officer who had actually been transferred to Dublin six months before the seizure had taken place. I knew this because I had replaced this officer on mobile duties after his transfer. Gerry went on to tell me what role I had played in the seizure. He told me that I had placed the mobile car in the garage and then cycled to my digs, which was correct. The subject of the second seizure then came up. He claimed that John Gerard Walsh had committed perjury in giving his evidence to the court. I told him that John Gerard was the straightest man I knew and would not allow anyone to say that he knowingly told lies in court. In truth, two offences had taken place on that occasion. The pigs seen passing through Dundalk had been pushed across the Border and the sows that were on the lorry in the shed had been imported, all in the same operation. It was an example of the efficiency of the smugglers involved.

My brother-in-law, Fr. Dan Fagan, had been ordained in the early fifties for the New Zealand mission. He served there and in the United States for many years before returning to get a parish in Armagh. While in New Zealand he became friendly with the Browne family especially with Bishop Denis and Fr. Michael, both of whom stayed with us while on a visit Ireland. Gerry McGeough, while on a trip to New Zealand, was introduced to Bishop Denis. On learning that Gerry came from Dundalk the bishop asked did he know me. It would have been interesting to hear his reply. Gerry gave me an account of his time in New Zealand and after one of these visits he gave me a photo of the Pope and Bishop Browne. Some years later I received an invitation to Gerry's 90th birthday to be held at the Lisdoo. This was not my scene but I attended and with Bishop Browne we wished Gerry a very happy birthday.

I am now happy in retirement reflecting on an interesting and satisfying career with ample time to pursue other interests but "Sin sceal fe leith".

12 | APPENDICES

APPENDIX 1 - DUTIES & REGULATIONS

Perhaps, at this juncture it might be of interest to look back and give a list of non-Revenue preventive work performed by Customs and Excise staff over the years. Surprisingly their work was not always confined to the obvious, that is the detection of smuggling. The following list is contained in the 21st Annual Report of the Revenue Commissioners (1946).

They were responsible for the prevention of importation of many goods including:

§ Obscene literature, pictures etc.
§ Advertisement of lotteries.
§ Foreign coins, other than gold or silver, and imitation coins.
§ Fictitious stamps and dies or instruments for making such stamps.
§ The plumage of birds, with certain exceptions
§ Prepared opium (on behalf of Dept of Justice).
§ Contraceptives.
   They were responsible for the prevention of the irregular importation of a number of items:
§ Explosives (on behalf of Dept of Justice).
§ Arms and ammunition (on behalf of Dept of Justice).
§ Dangerous drugs (on behalf of Dept of Justice).
§ Works infringing copyright in the State.
§ Sugar (on behalf of Dept of Industry and Commerce).
§ Therapeutic substances (on behalf of Dept of Local Government and Public Health).
§ Motor Vehicles prohibited under the Road Transport Act, 1935 (on behalf of Dept Industry & Commerce).
§ Pigs (on behalf of Dept of Agriculture).
§ Cattle, horses, asses, dogs and other animals, hay and

straw (on behalf of Dept of Agriculture).

§ Goods prohibited under the Emergency Powers Orders. They were responsible for the prevention of the irregular exportation of:

§ Arms and Ammunition (on behalf of Dept of Justice).

§ Dangerous drugs (on behalf of Dept of Justice).

§ Eggs (on behalf of Dept of Agriculture).

§ Sheepskin (on behalf of Dept of Industry and Commerce).

§ Archaeological objects.

§ Goods prohibited under the Agricultural Produce (cereals Act).

§ Scrap Iron (on behalf of Dept of Industry and Commerce).

§ Tobacco.

§ Goods prohibited under the Emergency Powers (Controls of Exports) Orders.

They were also responsible for the collection of passenger returns and certain other work under the Aliens Act (on behalf of the Dept of Justice).

There were numerous other regulations, which became effective subsequent to 1st April, 1923, and which involved addition to, or modification in, the non-Revenue preventive work of the Dept which were in force up to 1946. Some of which are listed below:

The Foot and Mouth Diseases Order, 1923; The Dairy Produce Act, 1924; The Firearms Act, 1925; The Importation of Dogs and Cats Order, 1929; The Censorship of Publications Act, 1929; The Agricultural Produce (Fresh Meat) Act, 1930; The Foot and Mouth Diseases (Movement of Animals from Northern Ireland) Order, 1931; The Road Transport Act, 1935; The Pigs and Bacon Act, 1935; The Poultry and Poultry Eggs (Importation) Order, 1938; Fruit (Regulation of Import) Order, 1938; Grass Seed (Regulation of Import) Order, 1938; The Emergency Powers (Exportation of Dead Poultry and Rabbits) Order, 1941; The

Emergency Powers (Purchase of Motor Lorries) Order, 1941; Apples (Regulation of Import) Order, 1941; Onions (Regulation of Import) Order, 1941; Live Goats (Regulation of Export) Order, 1942; Sugar (Prohibition of Import) Order, 1943; Scrap Iron (Prevention of Export) Order, 1943.

Appendix 2 -- Staff Association Officials & Report

Preventive Staff Association 1966-1972

Association's Officials and Representatives

President

Mr J. O'Shea

(Dundalk)

Hon. Gen. Secretary	Hon. Gen Treasurer	Research
Mr. David Mangan	Mr S. O'Cathasaigh	Mr R. O'Murchadha

Executive Council Members

Mr E. Cleary (Waterford)
Mr F. A. Hillen (Dundalk)
Mr. M. Mc Donald (Raphoe)
Mr. E.T. Mc Mahon (Monaghan)
Mr. Moran (Lifford)
Mr. S. Plunkett (Dublin Airport)

Representatives to Revenue Group of
Departmental Association and
Revenue Staff Panel:

Mr P. B. Fitzpatrick
Mr. D Mangan
Mr. S. Plunkett

Representatives to Custom & Excise
Benevolent Society
Mr J. Finnegan
Mr. M. O'Mara

Representatives to Civil Service
Benevolent Society
Mr J. Finnegan
Mr. M. C. Smith

Editorial:	Editorial Board	Delegate to Trade Union
"Customs Journal"	Mr. D. Mangan	Congress
Mr J.P. McGowan	Mr. D. O'Dowda	Mr. D. Mangan
	Mr. T.J. Walsh	

Revenue Departmental Council.   Appendix B.

Agreed Report No. 206.

(Meeting of 22 June, 1967).

Official Side: Mr. L. O'Muirgheasa, Director of
Establishments (Chairman) and
Messrs J.B. McCreesh, P. de Hógla and
P. Ó Délaigh (Secretary).

Staff Side: Mr. S. Ó Naonaigh Principal Staff
Representative, Mr. T. MacCarthaigh,
Mr. J. O'Shea and Miss M. Ní
Dhomhnalláin, (Secretary).

Claim that a special allowance be paid to mobile patrol crews.

(1)   The Staff Side said that their claim was for payment of a weekly
allowance of 10 hours overtime at weekday rates to members of mobile
patrol crews, irrespective of the actual number of weekday hours
worked. The allowance was claimed with effect from 6 May, 1967 inclusive.

(2)   The Staff Side said that mobile crews had been operating for many
years back. Following the relaxation in cross-border control at the
Frontier Posts with effect from 6 May, 1967 a greater reliance was now
being placed on mobile patrol crews. Consequently a very keen devotion
to duty and a high degree of initiative was now required from members
of the crews to ensure the success of the new arrangement. Moreover,
mobile crews were subject to many hazards and hardships, their hours
of duty were irregular and prolonged and they could not arrange their
leisure hours with any degree of certainty. The Staff Side said that
a similar allowance was payable to British atenguard mobile crews
working on similar duties in Northern Ireland. There was a strong
case, therefore, for conceding the claim. They estimated that the cost
of the allowance would be offset by the saving in overtime at the
Frontier Posts.

(3)   The Official Side said they recognised that recent developments
had resulted in a greater burden of responsibility for cross-border
control being laid to the mobile patrol crews and that the success of
these developments would largely depend on the devotion, initiative and
unremitting efforts of the crews. They were also satisfied that under the new

system it was desirable to provide an incentive for mobile patrol crews.
In the circumstances they were prepared to join in an agreed recommendation
that with effect from 6th May, 1967, a credit of 2 hours overtime per
day be paid to Preventive Staff in respect of each week day on which a
member of the Staff is employed on mobile patrol duties, subject to a
maximum credit of 10 hours per week. The credit will cover all
week-day overtime on mobile patrols including night credits. Payment
of overtime for attendances on Sundays and Public Holidays is not
affected.

Agreement was recorded accordingly and this report was adopted
by the Council.

Appendix 3 Seizure Samples

Year	Type of Goods	Import/Export
1951	Animal hides	Import
	Poultry	Export
	Eggs	Export
	Bicycles	Import
	Egg cases	Import
	Pigs	Export
	Cigarettes	Export
	Oxo cubes	Import
	Motor car battery	Import
	Sugar	Export
	Wire nails	Import
	Scrap lead	Export
	Motor car	Import
	Rags	Export
	33 loaves of bread	Export
	144 Lbs margarine	Export
	Carpet/felt	Import

Officers on duty during 1951 :-

Pat Langan, John Gerard Walsh, Tommy Woods, Jim O Shea,
John Lynch, James (Spud) Murphy, Frank Hillen, Sean Gallagher,
John King, Denis Farren.

Year	Type of Goods	Import/Export
1952	Fertilizer	Import
	Range/Irongates/Wire	Import
	Butter	Import
	Egg cases	Import
	Pigs	Import
	Razor blades (Blue Gilette)	Import
	Calf meal	Import
	Boots	Import
	Hides (£882 fine imposed)	Import

After 1951/52 most of the smuggling was Import

Year	Type of Goods	Import/Export
1953	Hens	Import
	Eggs	Import
	Ford V8 Motor car	Import
	Spark plugs (Champion)	Import
	Potatoes	Import
	Washing powder (Tide)	Import
	Nissan hut (in sections)	Import
	Day old chicks (Chickens destroyed by drowning)	Import
	Fertilizer	Import
	Fireworks	Import
	Drinking glasses	Import
	Onions	Import
	Tyres	Import

Year	Type of Goods	Import/Export
1954	Fertilizer	Import
	Egg cases	Import
	Pigs	Import
	Onions	Import
	Spark plugs	Import
	Batteries	Import
	Tyres	Import
	Soap powder	Import
	Meal	Import
	Twist tobacco	Import
	Potatoes	Import
	Grass seed	Import
	Fish (Cod)	Import
	Cigarettes	Import
	Cardigans (23)	Import

1954 was also the year of a celebrated assault case. Vince Dullaghan, who sold vegetables at the post office, was charged with assaulting Frank Millen. When the judge questioned Frank, who had more than a little boxing experience, how he defended himself, Frank replied that he parried with his left and crossed with his right. The judge immediately dismissed the assault case.

Year	Type of Goods	Import/Export
1955	Grass seed	Import
	Flake meal	Import
	Basic slag	Import
	Oxo cubes	Import
	Carrots	Import
	Apples	Import
	Cement	Import
	Razor blades (Gilette)	Import
	Pigs	Import
	Fertilizer	Import
	Zephyr car	Import
	Cotton thread	Import
	Sweets (Mars bars, spangles)	Import
	Suit lengths (13-3 ¾ yds each)	Import
	Second hand clothes	Import
	Cigarettes (30,000 Woodbines, 20,000 Players)	Export

Year	Type of Goods	Import/Export
1956	Oxo cubes	Import
	Blades	Import
	Cloth	Import
	Apples	Import
	Chicken meal	Import
	Day old chicks (2000 destroyed by drowning)	Import
	Sows	Import
	Sultanas/raisins	Import
	Breaches of TIP regs	

Year	Type of Goods	Import/Export
1957	Ford Pilot V8 car (sold for £27)	Import
	Oxo cubes	Import
	Butter (1/2 ton)	Import
	Cigarettes (80,000 woodbine, 40,000 players)	Import
	Bicycles	Import
	Oranges	Import
	Spark plugs	Import
	Hacksaw blades	Import
	Bicycle chains	Import
	Linoleum	Import

Year	Type of Goods	Import/Export
1958	Butter (1 ½ Cwt butter in Ford V8)	Import
	Remould tyres	Import
	Oxo cubes	Import

Year	Type of Goods	Import/Export
1959	Oxo cubes	Import
	Gin	Import
	Cigarettes	Import
	Grass seed	Import
	Tyres	Import
	Egg cases	Import
	Diesel engine	Import
	Butter	Import

Officers on duty :-

Pat Fitzpatrick, Jimmy Agnew
Eamonn Gribben, Charlie McGee

Year	Type of Goods	Import/Export
1960	Onions	Import
	1 ½ ton of Butter	Import
	Grass seed	Import
	Suits/Jackets (£950 fine)	Import
	Bedspreads (£300 fine)	Import

Officers on duty :-

Hugh Connolly, Pat Fitzpatrick, Jimmy Agnew (Drumbilla)

Colm Donaghy, Hughie Wynn, Frank Hillen
Vincent McMurrow, Liam Murphy, Joe Murray
Pat Langan, Spud Murphy, Charlie McCarthy (Mobiles)

Tim Stack, Donal Hallissey (Relief staff)

Jim O Shea (Tiger)

C.P.O. John Gerard Walsh

Jimmy Walsh, Johnny Gordon, Paddy Bennett
Peadar Clancy, Frank Hayes (Ball)

Year	Type of Goods	Import/Export
1961	27 x 28 Lbs butter	Import
	36 x 56 Lbs butter (2 £100 fines)	Import
	3 Tons butter	Import
	5 Cwt butter	Import

Officers on duty –

Jim O Shea, Hughie Wynne, Donal Cotter
Francie Mangan, Paul Brohan, Seamus Cullen
Bill Whelan, Matt Twomey, Mick McGlynn

Year	Type of Goods	Import/Export
1962	Matches (16 gross)	Import
	2 x 56 Lbs butter	Import
	Electric motors	Import
	7 ton of Potatoes	Export
	2 ½ ton of Potatoes	Export
	1 ¾ ton butter (100 x 28Lbs)	Import
	3900 Dozen eggs	Import
	1 ¾ Cwt butter	Import
	5 ton butter (200 x 56 Lbs)	Import

Officers on duty –

Pat Larkin, J. Travers, D. Cotter
H.P. Wynne

Liam Corbet, Tony O Brien (Castleblaney)

Donie Collins, John O Brien, P.J. Costello,
Pat Larkin (Dundalk)

Year	Type of Goods	Import/Export
1963	Rice Horsebox	Import
	5 pigs	Import
	12 x 56 Lbs butter	Import
	Blankets (97 pairs)	Import
	Coffee tables	Import
	Handbags	Import
	Rugs	Import
	Cutlery and Lamps	Import
	Coffee tables (108)	Import
	Store cattle (13)	Import

Officers on duty –

John Lynch, Mick Goss, Sean de Faoite
John O Brien

Year	Type of Goods	Import/Export
1964	Motor Lorry Tyres	Import
	20 Eiderdowns	Import
	26 Blankets	Import
	Television	Import
	Rugs	Import
	Sheets	Import
	Ball Point Pens (4 gross)	Import
	Live eels (23 boxes)	Import
	Coffee tables (108)	Import
	Store cattle (13)	Import
	Officers on duty –	
	Mick Crowley	

Year	Type of Goods	Import/Export
1965	Blankets (25)	Import
	Sheets (24)	Import
	Radios (6)	Import
	Potatoes (8 ½ ton)	Import
	Potatoes (10 ton)	Import
	Potatoes (10 ½ ton)	Import
	Potatoes (10 ton)	Import
	Caravans	Import
	Eels (108)	Import
	Store cattle (13)	Import
	Some new staff names –	
	C O Crowe, Pat McLoughlin, Gerry O Connor	
	Bill Meehan, Mick Crowley	

Year	Type of Goods	Import/Export
1966	No seizures of note in 1966	
	Some staff names appearing on seizure records –	
	Seamus O Croinin, Tom O Loughlin, P Gannahty	
	S Mac Roibin, Liam O Mahony, J J Mooney	
	A W O Reilly, Michael McPhadon, J Clifford	
	John Hanley, Pat Twomey, Sean Heaney	

Year	Type of Goods	Import/Export
1967	Potatoes (9 ton)	Import
	Onions (200 bag)	Import
	Barley (11 ½ ton)	Import
	Butter (1 ton)	Import
	Butter (5 ½ ton)	Import
	Staff names appearing for the first time –	
	Pat Kelly, Tom Geary, Mick Quelly	
	James E McDonagh, P R Griffee,	
	Tom Small, J J Bradley, Colm Donnellan,	
	J V Sullivan, Felix Loughnan	

Year	Type of Goods	Import/Export
1968	Lorry Engines (3)	Import
	Used lorry tyres (700)	Import
	Spark plugs	Import
	Butter (903 lbs)	Import
	Bacon	Import
	Hams	Import
	Dog Food	Import
	Lorry wheels	Import
	Potatoes	Export
	Fireworks	Import

New Officers –

Gerry Ahern, S.A. MacTaorish, C. Harvey
Paddy Haughey

Year	Type of Goods	Import/Export
1969	Pantyhose (200 lbs)	Import
	Smoked fish (Cod)	Import
	Sheets (175 prs)	Import
	Pillow cases (104 doz)	Import
	Jeans	Import
	4,000 Cigarettes	Import
	5 galls Spirits	Import
	Laurie Horse Box	Import
	Blankets	Import
	Quilts	Import
	Bedspreads	Import
	Potatoes (4 ½ ton)	Import
	Candlewick (100)	Import
	Bacon (3 ½ ton)	Import
	Butter (2 ton)	Import
	Lorry Engines (2 perkins, 1 AEC)	Import
	Grain (31 ton 3 cwt)	Import

One of the biggest cigarette seizures took place this year. On
18/11/69 the M/V Fredel offloaded 200,000 Pall Mall, 305,000
Players and 310,000 Benson & Hedges.

New Officers –

Eoin Prunty, William Crerand, Charlie O Brien

Year	Type of Goods	Import/Export
1970	Butter (1 ton)	Import
	Cement	Import
	Gents trousers (43)	Import
	Spark plugs (500)	Import
	Drive Couplings (4)	Import
	Pigs (14)	Import

New Officers –

Rodger Coffey, Sean P O Brien, Denis Leahy
B.B. White, Hugh McCrudden, Mick Hannon
M.O.Cuirc

Year	Type of Goods	Import/Export
1970	Butter (1 ton)	Import
	Cement	Import
	Gents trousers (43)	Import
	Spark plugs (500)	Import
	Drive Couplings (4)	Import
	Pigs (14)	Import

New Officers: *

Rodger Coffey, Sean P O'Brien, Denis Leahy, B.B. White, Hugh McCrudden, Mick Hannon, M.O Cuirc

Year	Type of Goods	Import/Export
1971	Cigarettes (650,000 B&H, 90,000 Players)	Import
	M/v Merlin 11/05/71	
	Cigarettes (375,000 Players, 34 Cs Whiskey, 26 Cs Brandy)	Import
	Soldiers Point 13/12/71	
	5000 Cigarettes	
	11 4/6 galls Brandy	Import
	Ex Marie Both	
	Butter (10 cwt)	Import

New Officers: *

Aiden Mulrooney

Year	Type of Goods	Import/Export
1972	Onions	Import
	Apples	Import
	Bacon (36 sidm)	Import
	Onions	Import
	Barley (16 ton)	Import
	Radios	Import
	Watches	
	Radios	Import
	Lorry	Import

This year saw the start of big time 'Radio' smuggling by itinerants.

New Officers: *

Martin Kerins

138